"*GodSense* is one of the most immediately accessible and therefore relevant devotional books I have ever read. The wisdom herein is at once both philosophic and pithy, principled and practical. This is the book for anyone hungering for a deeper everyday relationship with God."

Dr. Rex Rogers
President, Cornerstone University

"*GodSense* is a wonderful collection of immensely practical devotionals which are clear, concise, readable, theologically insightful, and spiritually inspiring. I found myself frequently stopping to write quotes in the margins of my Bible for later reflection and implementation."

Dr. Bill Rudd
Senior pastor, Calvary Church
Trustee, Cedarville University

The GodSense Devotional

52 Weeks to a Transformed Life

To Suzanne—

May God bless your life in His presence!

Ps. 84:1-2

The GodSense Devotional

52 Weeks to a Transformed Life

BEVERLY VAN KAMPEN

with prayers written by Margery Lembke

FaithWalk
PUBLISHING
Grand Haven, Michigan

Published by FaithWalk Publishing
333 Jackson Street, Grand Haven, Michigan 49417
faithwalkpub.com

Printed in the United States of America

09 08 07 06 05 04   7 6 5 4 3 2 1

Library of Congress Control Number: 2003113249
ISBN: 0-9724196-6-7   (pbk.: alk. paper)

This book is dedicated to my two daughters,
Andrea Masvero and Tarah Boeve,
both of whom have taught me more about
walking with God than I ever could have
learned without them.

Acknowledgments

I would like to acknowledge and thank the following individuals who were very helpful and instrumental in bringing this book to publication:

First, thank you to the women in the Bible studies in which I participate. You have kept me focused on God's word and accountable to its teaching.

Second, thank you to Dirk Wierenga and Louann Werksma of FaithWalk Publishing for their patient guidance and creative working with me throughout the editing and publication process.

Third, thank you to my husband Warren who prays for me, provides for me, and encourages me in all of my writing and teaching endeavors. Without his loving and enthusiastic support, the privilege of authorship would never have been mine.

Beverly Van Kampen
October 2003

Contents

Introduction

This devotional is written for people who want a deeper sense of God in their lives. Some of you who have picked up this book have been Christians for many years, but your relationship with God never "took off," or it has grown stale. This book is for you. It will revitalize your walk with God and will refresh your spirit.

Others of you are exploring Christianity and relationship with God. You may be fledgling believers with very little Bible knowledge or church background. This book is for you.

Engage one principle at a time and allow the Spirit of God to teach you and to draw you closer to him as you begin to understand how you, as a mere human being, can relate in a personal and intimate way with the God of the universe. You're in for great surprises—all of them good!

If you need more help getting started, you might begin by reading the Epilogue, which will guide you to an initial relationship with your loving creator.

There are two ways in which we experience true GodSense. The first is by *knowing about* God. We, as his followers, need to learn what he has revealed to us about himself in the Bible, in the world around us, and through others who believe in him and follow him, too. This book is centered around the Bible because that is where we find truth and where we find the power to live our lives as God directs.

But, there is more to God than knowing lots of facts about him. There is a *sensing of* God that many long for and find inaccessible. This book will help you to *know* God and who he is; it will also lead you, step-by-step, down a path that will allow you to *sense* God as he speaks to your soul and draws you into a closer relationship with him.

I am on that path myself. I grew up going to church, memorizing Bible passages, studying Bible books and stories, and being actively involved in Sunday School, Bible School, summer Bible camp, youth choirs, and various youth activities. I knew a lot about God, but there came a point in my life when knowing all these facts and even relating to God in prayer, Bible study, church attendance, and service were not enough. I wanted more. I wanted to feel him, to sense him, to learn to love him, and to receive his love in return.

I began my journey to a vital, growing relationship with God, first of all, by reading some early Christian authors who, by describing their relationship with God, were describing exactly what I wanted to experience myself. I read, among others, Teresa of Avila, Brother Lawrence, Thomas a'Kempis, Thomas Kelly, and Julian of Norwich. Later I discovered more recent contemplative writers such as Evelyn Underhill and Thomas Merton. These writers had discovered a side of God that I had not yet experienced. They knew him in a meditative, experiential way that I longed for.

One thing these writers seemed to have in common was a consistent and focused practice of what we have come to define as the *spiritual disciplines*. These include prayer, meditation, worship, solitude, simplicity, study, fasting, and confession, among others. I began, with a certain amount of hesitation, but with an equal amount of anticipation, to practice these various disciplines. A greater sense of the presence of God grew within me. I began to discover how much he loves me, how much he desires an ongoing personal relationship with me, and how many ways he sought to encourage my intimacy with him.

At one point, it seemed that I had hit a roadblock. There was something between God and me and it seemed to keep me from a fuller, deeper, more meaningful relationship with him. All I knew was that I wanted to love him more than I did and I wanted to experience his love more than I was. God seemed to tell me, on more than one occasion during times of prayer, that I needed to see a Christian counselor. In fact, a name came into my mind of the very counselor I was supposed to see. After repeatedly asking God to break through to my heart and after repeated answers that I sensed from him that I needed to see this psychologist, I finally followed God's direction and made the appointment.

The initial meeting was followed by a year-long series of sessions in which I discovered that this particular counselor had followed a spiritual path that was parallel to the one I was on. He had found a vital, loving, and growing relationship with his creator, but only after he had worked through a number of emotional blocks that he had carried with him from childhood. I had many of the same issues and found that my time with him helped me to understand myself better which helped me to relate more freely and openly with God. His counsel was a turning point in my ability to sense God. God had not changed, but my ability to receive him had. And I had learned an important lesson: We need each other in order to grow fully into GodSense. We need to share each other's stories—both our successes and our failures—and to learn from one another.

I continue to read good books, to practice various spiritual disciplines, and to communicate consistently with God. It is an exhilarating journey that grows more vibrant and more meaningful as I move forward. One of the greatest joys is being able to share what I am learning with others around me. I have been able to teach Bible study groups and retreat sessions and to share God's message with various church groups.

The writing of *GodSense* has grown out of what I have discovered through relationships that have developed as I have talked with others about walking with God. I have found that people want to know how to do it. They want to know how to hear God's voice.

They want to know how to please him. They want to know how to receive his love and his great gifts of grace. They want to serve him. But they need to know *how*.

This book is designed to help the reader know *how* to sense God, how to approach him, and how to walk with him in loving relationship throughout a lifetime and into eternity.

All I can do in these pages is to share what has worked for me. The more I read and study, the more I realize that what has worked for me has worked for many, many other God-followers throughout history. It will work for you, too.

The book presents fifty-two principles and is designed to allow you to engage with one principle each week for one year. As you read the teaching, meditate on the Scripture, study God's Word, and apply these principles to your life, you will find that your heart is turned toward God to a greater and greater degree. You will find that as you begin to focus on him, your understanding of him becomes clearer, you receive his love more fully, and your sense of him and his presence with you grows deeper each day. It's not a complicated path, but it's not an easy one either. It will take commitment and resolve to see it through, but the rewards are eternal and beyond description.

By the time you finish this study, there are ten key statements that I pray you will be able to make. If you can honestly state them and keep them in front of you as you move closer and closer to God, you will have developed a GodSense that will propel you toward intimate relationship with him. Those statements, which correspond with the themes of the principles in this book, are:

1. I choose to follow God.
2. I learn to know and accept truth.
3. I am being changed from within.
4. I trust God.
5. I live in this moment.
6. I believe God and act on that belief.
7. I communicate with God.
8. I worship my Creator.
9. I have discovered joy.
10. I live a meaning-filled life.

You will find these statements written on a page at the end of this book as a reminder of our goals as we pursue a life of greater connection to God.

Many of the passages presented for meditation are taken from *The Message*, which is a translation of the Bible from original texts, but which uses modern English language in order to give a fresh, more understandable approach to the meaning of the Scripture. I trust you will look at these passages with an open mind and take to heart the message that they convey. Other Scriptures, unless otherwise noted, are taken from the Holy Bible New International Version, a commonly accepted translation used in many of our churches today.

At the end of each of the teaching on each of the principles, you will find a prayer that has been written by Margery Lembke, a dear friend who has been my mentor in this journey toward knowing God on a more experiential level. Marge and I have taken and led several spiritual retreats together and meet regularly in order to share with one another what God is doing in our lives. We have been privileged to share together in some teaching opportunities and find that God has richly blessed our efforts. When the editor of *GodSense* suggested that it might be helpful to the reader to have prayers throughout the book that would assist with a heart connection to our heavenly Father, there was no doubt in my mind who should write those prayers. I know of no individual who is more conversant with God and more able to introduce others to him through prayer. I thank Marge for her willingness to participate in this project and believe that you, the reader, will be greatly blessed by what she has contributed. So, I invite you to read, to savor the God-truths that you discover in these pages, and to experience God in a new and living way. You will never be sorry that you took the first step down this path. It is the path to truth, to life, and to God.

Instructions

MONDAY

Each week we will study a principle relating to spiritual growth. That principle will be introduced and explained on Monday. Keep your Bible nearby as we go through these studies each week.

TUESDAY

You will be guided into a meditation on a Bible verse or passage related to the weekly principle. Suggestions for effective meditation are as follows:

Sit in a comfortable chair with both feet flat on the floor. Place your arms on the arm of the chair or place your hands on your lap. Many prefer having the palms facing upward as if in anticipation of receipt of a response from God.

Relax your body. One by one tense your muscle groups beginning with your feet and working your way up to the top of your head. After you tense them, release them and allow the muscles to remain relaxed. Make sure you have released all the tensed muscles in your face and neck. Sit with your jaw relaxed and lips slightly open.

Now focus on your breathing. Visualize the breath entering your body and leaving it as you inhale, hold the breath, and then slowly exhale. Do this several times until you are relaxed, oxygenated, and focused solely on breathing.

By now, your mind should be disengaged from random thoughts. Think of a quiet place of natural serenity or imagine Christ sitting beside you.

Then begin to concentrate your thoughts on a word or phrase from the passage of Scripture given for that day. Allow God to speak to you through your thoughts.

After the meditation is finished, write down anything that comes to your mind during this time of quiet before God.

WEDNESDAY AND THURSDAY

Further teaching will be provided concerning the principle under consideration.

FRIDAY

You will be encouraged to engage in a personal Bible reading/study on a particular passage of Scripture related to the principle. Questions are provided to stimulate your study, and space is available in which to write what you discover in the text.

Instructions

You will be asked to think about how the weekly principle can be applied to your life. Key questions or thoughts will be presented with opportunity for you to respond in the space provided.

SUNDAY

This day is devoted to prayer. A prayer will be provided, which you are invited to pray. You may choose to continue with spoken or written prayers of your own. Space is provided for writing prayers or any thoughts that may come to you during your time of focused prayer.

GodSense Principles

1. The more we simplify our lives, the deeper we can go into the richness of relationships and the satisfaction of spiritual connection.

2. God reveals his will only to those who love him enough to do whatever he says.

3. Hearing and obeying God frees us from the tyranny of our own resourcefulness.

4. A heart commitment allows us to take the step in front of us without needing to know the details of the journey.

5. God lavishly rewards a life of humble obedience.

6. Once we stop running from truth and turn, instead, to seek it, it will be found.

7. When we think we have discovered truth, we need to look one layer deeper to see if what we have found is truth from God or a lie from man.

8. Truth revealed is truth revered.

9. God's truth is a mystery revealed and a power released.

10. The goal of my soul
    Is to cling to my King!

11. True life that is fresh and free and full is found only in undistracted connection to God.

12. Turning toward God puts me face-to-face with him. He draws me closer one step at a time.

13. Just for today, choose to have an attitude of joy and hope. Tomorrow making that choice will be easier.

14. What seems like a risk to me is no risk at all under the watchful and guiding eye of my heavenly Father.

15. God's healing touch can reach only to the buried pains that we are willing to expose. The rest remain hidden and unhealed.

16. Our personal wholeness and our devotion to God are intricately and irreversibly intertwined.

17. The life of the Spirit does not mean perfection, but it means continually moving toward that goal.

18. In order to come to the end of our lives in satisfied fulfillment, we must stay in touch with God's Spirit within us today.

19. Our faith is effective only if the one in whom we have placed it is both powerful and loving.

20. Having a problem we cannot solve will either turn us bitter or turn us to God.

21. Getting to know God is getting to know he is trustworthy.

22. We don't have to have all the answers.
    We just have to know the one who does.

23. Our suffering is the stethoscope through which we hear the heartbeat of God.

24. Real life begins when we learn to experience the present moment.

25. Fears, worries, and regrets are like clouds that cover the beauty of our lives.

26. We would be foolish to focus only on the present moment if we did not believe that someone wiser and stronger than we are is in charge of our lives.

27. If we think that God doesn't like to have fun, we have never really looked at a duck-billed platypus.

28. We don't want to get to the end of our lives and find out that we missed living!

29. Living by faith is as unnatural to humans as is swimming under water.

30. We don't have to be perfect; we just have to be his.

31. God breathes peace into my soul.

32. We can know with confidence that we will become what God has always had in mind for us to be.

33. Hope is the light that keeps us moving forward even when we are walking through darkness and desperation.

34. You are God's favorite child!

35. The greatest gift of love we can give to anyone is our time.

36. God is not hiding. Go ahead and get to know him.

37. No personal sacrifice we make for God will go unrewarded.

38. Find a teacher and learn all you can. Then find a student and teach all you know.

39. The gifts of devotion we give to God open the passageway to heaven so that his love can flow freely back to us.

40. Our lives must be about God alone, not God and... .

41. Adoration is an outward expression of our inward devotion to God.

42. Worship that doesn't move us probably won't move God either!

43. Love, by its very nature, must give gifts!

44. Worship shared is worship magnified.

45. Worship is a gift we give to God.
    Intimacy and blessings are its rewards.

46. God loves to celebrate!

47. God came to earth to let us know that our happiness is very important to him.

48. Joy sneaks up when you least expect it.

49. The true joy of God meets our deepest soul-needs.

50. It's easier to love mankind than it is to love the human beings who share our daily lives!

51. Have the time of your life! But do so in light of the eternity of your life.

52. We don't know how exhilarating it is to fly until we take off!

My *GodSense* Life

I choose to follow God.

I learn to know and accept truth.

I am being changed from within.

I trust God.

I live in this moment.

I believe God and act on that belief.

I communicate with God.

I worship my Creator.

I have discovered joy.

I live a meaning-filled life.

Longing for the Simple Life

P r i n c i p l e   # 1

The more we simplify our lives, the deeper we can go into the richness of relationships and the satisfaction of spiritual connection.

More than a century and a half ago, Henry David Thoreau was dissatisfied with the complicated nature of his life and he retreated to now famous Walden Pond where his main goal was to simplify his life. Although many of those who knew him at that time considered him to be a peculiar radical, he learned much about himself and the world in which he existed by retreating from the madness of the culture around him. In writing about his experience he advised all of us to "Simplify, simplify, simplify." We may agree that he had great insight, but have we taken that advice?

In fact, for most of us, our lives are more complicated than ever. We have thrown ourselves into trying new methods for effective living, systems of organization, 12-step self-help programs, and labor-saving devices, all of which promise to simplify our lives and none of which seem to do so. We try to manage careers, raise children, purchase new homes, and get involved in personal support groups.

Besides our insatiable need to juggle multiple tasks at one time, we also have bought into the concept that more stuff will make our lives easier. But instead of possessions simplifying our lives and enabling them to run more efficiently, we often find that the things we own tend to own us. First we need to learn how to use them, and then we need to maintain them, repair them, and eventually replace them with newer, bigger, and better.

Isn't there something deep within you that desires simplicity, less clutter, fewer demands on your time, and an inner peace that allows you to relate on a deeper level with God and with those around you? We long for rest for our bodies and for our souls, but we experience no inner peace and can identify no path by which it can be found. While we are juggling all the various demands of our lives, we are frustrated at the level of our spiritual growth. We can't even hear the "still, small voice" inside of us, whispering that there is a better way. A simpler way.

The first step is to reflect on what is important in our lives. Then we will begin to see how making God our only goal will cause all other priorities to fall neatly into line. Before we know it, we will find ourselves walking freely and joyfully in the wide open spaces that God has provided.

TUESDAY

Meditation

These verses will be the focus of our thoughts this week. Read them and take a few moments today to meditate on God's message to you.

"Are you tired? Worn out? Burned out on religion? Come to me. Get away with me and you'll recover your life. I'll show you how to take a real rest. Walk with me and work with me—watch how I do it. Learn the unforced rhythms of grace. I won't lay anything heavy or ill-fitting on you. Keep company with me and you'll learn to live freely and lightly."
(Matthew 11:28–30 *The Message*)

Journal

WEDNESDAY

Thoughts for today:

Jesus is our example of the simple life to which God has called each of us. He learned a basic carpenter's trade, owned no home, had no means of transportation except for an occasional borrowed boat or donkey, and apparently was able to carry everything he owned with him as he walked from place to place. He had no formal education other than the religious education that was given to all Jewish boys as they began to prepare for adulthood.

As Jesus taught, people listening noted that he spoke truth with authority—and with simplicity. He took the hundreds of laws that the religious leaders had developed over the centuries and boiled them down to two: (1) Love God with all your heart, mind, soul, and strength; and (2) love your neighbor as yourself. Jesus showed us in this down-to-the-basics summary that he was not one to unnecessarily complicate the living out of our spiritual lives.

As we study Jesus' life, we discover that there were times when he, too, got tired. These were the times when he had to withdraw to be alone with his Father. If Jesus, the perfect God-Man, acknowledged the need for simple communion with God, will we need less? These daily times of quiet will grow us spiritually and will enable us to have a simple, uncluttered heart even in the middle of our busy lives.

THURSDAY

Thoughts for today:

The authority of Jesus' teaching and his life grew out of its very simplicity—especially his simple and unwavering obedience to the direction of his Father in heaven. I think of a couple of teachers I had who communicated clearly the lessons I needed to learn. Both of them were calm in spirit, simple in lifestyle, and seemed to teach me only a small portion of all that they knew. I felt that the very quietness of their natures concealed a depth that would not have been there if they were more frenetic personalities such as many of us experience today. I imagine that Jesus' early teaching style was much the same way. His very quiet self-assurance conveyed a depth that a louder, more forceful approach would not have portrayed.

We will want to think of ways we can make our lives less cluttered and more streamlined. But before we deal with that issue, let's acknowledge that simplicity is an attitude that, over time and practice, becomes a way of life. Throwing out may be part of what you need to do, but let's start with the attitude of simplicity before we get to the nitty-gritty of streamlined lives.

In these first few weeks we will look at the invitation to do things God's way, following the pattern Jesus has set. If we accept that invitation, simplicity will naturally follow. We will breathe freer and easier.

FRIDAY

Reading God's message
Luke 1:46–55

Mary, the mother of Jesus, came from a simple family and lived a simple life. We find, however, that she was totally devoted to God and followed him in humble obedience even when he asked her to do something very hard—to bear the stigma of conceiving a child out of wedlock and to bring into this world the Messiah who would not be understood and who would, in fact, suffer throughout his life and then die an ignominious death. Mary's heart of simple, humble obedience is evident when, after the angel appeared to her, she sang the song of praise to God found in this passage.

Spend some time reading that passage today and thinking about what it teaches you about Mary's heart.

Journal

SATURDAY

For   personal   reflection

What is one thing you can do today that will eliminate a distraction and create some time and space in your life for God?

_____

_____

As you visualize a simpler life, how do you see yourself relating differently to the people around you?

_____

_____

_____

SUNDAY

Prayer

O Lord, my Lord, give me that one unbreakable thread that keeps me connected to love, which is you, Lord Jesus. Thank you for making it simple and uncomplicated. I just choose you.

My prayer:

_____

_____

_____

_____

_____

Longing for the Simple Life

P r i n c i p l e   # 2

God reveals his will only to those who love him enough to do whatever he says.

Who knew more about how Model-T's ran than Henry Ford? He designed them. He made them. He knew how to make their engines rumble happily as they motored down the paths in Detroit. It is a good idea for us to remember that our master designer knows us better than we know ourselves, and his direction fine tunes our lives so that we can operate in true freedom and power. If we look to him for guidance throughout each day, we know that

- he will never give us more to do than we can get done.
- he will never ask us to do something we are not capable of doing.
- he will not ask us to buy something we cannot afford.
- he will not want us to own things we do not need.
- he will not get us in over our heads in any area of our lives.

Many of us get stuck in trying to know what God's plan for us is. If Jesus were sitting across the table from us right now and asked us to do something—anything—we would do it without hesitation. It would be clear to us what he wants. We want to please him, and we trust that what he asks us to do has significance in some way. But he is not visible to us in bodily form and, therefore, his directions are often not clear to us.

The most obvious place to learn what it is that God would have us do is in the Bible. The Bible is full of directions for us. How long has it been since we studied the Ten Commandments to find out how we should conduct our lives? If it has been awhile, and if we are really serious about obedience to God, this would be a good place to begin. A follow-up study would be to dig into the Sermon on the Mount (Matthew 5–7). In this sermon, Jesus tells us that following him involves our attitudes and motives and not just our actions. Are we obeying everything that Jesus taught in this famous, but often ignored, sermon?

Jesus was explaining to those who followed him why it was necessary for him to come. We couldn't live the God-expected life without his willingness to come to earth, communicate God's directions to us, and let us know that although we have failed to measure up to God's requirements, he is willing to take care of things for us. We just need to let him.

TUESDAY

Meditation

Think of God as a great and willing teacher. He wants you to know him, to know his will, to understand his loving desires for you to have a meaningful life with joy at its very center. Read and meditate on this verse which forms the basis of our study together this week.

"He wakens me morning by morning, wakens my ear to listen like one being taught."

(Isaiah 50:4b)

Journal

WEDNESDAY

Thoughts for today:

God is a communicative personality and he is talking to us all the time. He sometimes speaks to our hearts and gives specific directions for our lives. We need to slow down and be still so that we can hear what he has to say. This is not some concept that applies only to the hyper-spiritual. God speaks to all of his children; we simply need to take the time to hear and cherish his messages to us.

Sometimes his voice will urge us to change direction, serve another, adjust an attitude, repent of a sin, or share the message of his word with someone else. Often these urgings will come through our own thought processes and, therefore, we end up trying to determine if it really was God's voice we heard. When we are not sure, there are some steps we can take to confirm God's direction.

First, we should evaluate the circumstances in which we felt we heard the command. If we sense a direction from God when we are in an attitude of prayer and/or meditation and have blocked out distracting influences from our minds, it is safe to assume that the direction has come from the Holy Spirit. But, because we do not always hear God clearly, we will need to confirm the message we have received through Scripture, through a friend's guidance, and through circumstances of our lives.

THURSDAY

Thoughts for today:

If we sense that God is giving us direction, there are three sources for confirmation of the message we are hearing:

Scripture. Is the instruction consistent with the word of God and with what it reveals about the character of God? If so, we can follow it safely. We also may find that a passage of Scripture will confirm his direction or will give us instructions concerning how to carry it out.

Spiritual friend. If you do not have such a friend in your life, seek one out. Then, whenever you are in doubt about the clarity of God's message to you, call your friend for insight. God loves to have his children work together.

Circumstances. One time when I was praying early on a Sunday morning, I felt God was directing me to undertake a modified fast. When I went to our morning church service an hour later, the pastor preached that worldly pleasures or cravings often distract us from tasting of God himself. Later that afternoon, I picked up a book I was reading and the chapter I read had an entire section on fasting. God had confirmed his message!

If we think God is talking to us, we don't want to ignore him! We listen to his voice and then verify, by one of these ways, his message to us. Once we know with certainty what it is that he wants us to do, faithful obedience becomes the next logical step.

FRIDAY

Reading God's message

John 4:43–54

As you read this passage, focus on the reaction of the father to the words of Jesus. What does this tell you about how we should learn to respond when we receive a message or a word from God. How well do we take God at his word?

Journal

SATURDAY

For personal reflection

Quietly bow your head before God and ask him if there is a specific direction he has for you today. Then listen, focusing on him and his great love for you.

Write down anything that comes to your mind, trusting that the message is from God. If you have doubts, confirm the message with a mature Christian friend. If the message is confirmed, do whatever it is God has asked you to do.

If you hear nothing, don't be concerned. Ask him the same question tomorrow. Eventually his voice will break through to your heart. If you hear a direction from God, write it here:

_____

_____

_____

_____

SUNDAY

Prayer

My Father, I will not make any journey without you for you are the way that I have chosen to go. Your praise will continually be on my lips. I will lean on your guidance and your grace. In Jesus' holy name. Amen.

My prayer:

_____

_____

_____

_____

_____

Knowing What God Wants

P r i n c i p l e   # 3

Hearing and obeying God frees us from the tyranny of our own resourcefulness.

When God speaks to us through prayer or through the Holy Spirit, we must quickly respond. He expects nothing less.

I would like to share two examples from my own life of the kind of obedience he desires—the first is a time when I obeyed right away; the second is a time when I asked him to allow me to obey on my own timing. You will see from these examples that when I obeyed, I benefited. When I did not, it brought unnecessary difficulty into my life because God knew before he asked for my obedience what would be best for me.

I had been sensing that God wanted me to spend time in writing. I didn't know what he wanted me to write or for whom, but he seemed to be saying that I should write. So I attended a writers' conference and began to journal in earnest while waiting for direction to come. In the middle of my writing, I had an urgent call from an out-of-state friend who was having trouble with a young adult son who was making bad decisions that would affect the rest of his life. She despaired that she had failed as a mother. We talked, but it seemed that there was no way my words of comfort could reach her. So, I stopped the writing I was working on, and I wrote her a letter instead. Some time later she disclosed that the message of that letter was life-changing for her. It is a letter she still carries with her.

Then I kept getting direction to write letters: one to a woman in my Bible study group who was struggling with spiritual growth, another to a man at work dealing with issues in his marriage, one to each of my parents, and others still that I won't list individually here.

I concluded that maybe all God wanted me to write was letters. What I discovered in this process is that he wanted my obedience more than he wanted the great American novel or any exegesis on his word. The letters have been my training ground—not in writing, but in obedience. Willingness to follow his direction is more important than what we actually produce. That sometimes is a difficult concept for us to accept, but it is a principle of great importance in God's kingdom.

TUESDAY

Meditation

How are you doing in your spiritual walk? This verse gives you some ways to measure your spiritual condition. What are you doing well? Where do you want to see improvement? Ask God to change you in accordance with his perfect plan for you to become all that he wants you to be.

"The one who keeps God's word is the person in whom we see God's mature love. This is the only way to be sure we're in God. Anyone who claims to be intimate with God ought to live the same kind of life Jesus lived."
(I John 2:5–6 *The Message*)

Journal

WEDNESDAY

Thoughts for today:

There was a time when God called and I hesitated. God was telling me it was time for me to leave my full-time job. My husband and I agreed, after much prayer, that October would be my last month of work. When I discussed the issue with my employers, they suggested that I stay through December 31 on a reduced-time basis. I agreed.

Now, why would I agree to that? God had confirmed that I should be done working by the end of October. God did not strike me dead, he did not act mad, he (I think) just shook his great head and wondered why, after he had been so clear in his leading, I did not simply obey.

I would have been better off doing exactly what God had asked. Just days after I would have been done with my work, my 22-year-old daughter was diagnosed with cancer. For the next seven months she underwent surgery, chemotherapy, and radiation. For the first two months of those treatments, I juggled her care and my concern for her with my work responsibilities. If I had obeyed God's perfect timing, there would have been no juggling.

God knew that I would have been better off had I simply followed his perfect timetable. Obedience is hard partly because our own rationalizations seem to make compromise acceptable. Instead, God asks that we trust him and not rely on our own limited understanding.

THURSDAY

Thoughts for today:

Obeying God is not restrictive—it is freeing and, in that freedom, we will find a refreshing simplicity of life. As Jesus explained to the Jewish questioners in John 8, we either will know the truth of God and be free, or we will be enslaved to sin. There is no middle ground. Which boss would you rather answer to: self or God? Which will most likely be seeking your best good?

Obedience to God frees us from our own drives, our defense mechanisms, our need to acquire, our need to have the approval of others, and the covering up of our failures and sins. Seeking God and obeying him frees us from all the entanglements that complicate our lives so that, instead of being all tied up and stressed out, we walk about in wide open spaces where we can live and move in accordance with God's plan for our lives.

God never planned for us to be enslaved to this world or to our own agendas; his plan is for us to be free to follow him and pursue a friend-to-friend relationship with him. Obedience to God is much lighter than the burden of our own plans and the enslavement to sin that controls us if we have not yielded ourselves to God. Obeying him is not a sacrifice. Obedience is in our own best interest!

FRIDAY

Reading God's message

Psalm 119:41–48

Read these verses from one of the great psalms concerning God's word and our responses to it. List all the ways in which we are blessed and prosper when we are obedient to what God teaches.

Journal

SATURDAY

For personal reflection

Is there a sin or a habit in your life that you know displeases God?

Is there a relationship in your life that God is asking you to give up?

Is there someone whose forgiveness you need to seek? Or someone you need to forgive?

Do you have an attitude that needs to be changed?

If so, pray a prayer of confession, asking that God will forgive your sin, free you from its power, and enable you to walk in the freedom of unblocked connection to him. List the things you prayed about:

_____

_____

_____

SUNDAY

Prayer

Give me your grace, Father, to yield to this compelling love that wants to free me to be the person you created me to be. I will wait with expectant joy. Amen.

My prayer:

_____

_____

_____

_____

_____

Being What God Wants

P r i n c i p l e   # 4

A heart commitment allows us to take the step in front of us without needing to know the details of the journey.

We are planners by nature and want to see the end before we begin. God usually doesn't work that way, and I believe there is a reason. He wants us to trust him. If we could see the end of the story, we would not have to be walking by faith, and faith is a very big thing with God. So he asks us to make the heart commitment to obey the instruction in front of us right now and then to trust him to reveal the next step and the next as we move through our lives.

Think about Joseph whose story is told in the Book of Genesis. God gave him dreams as a young man about his brothers bowing down to him. God didn't give Joseph any details about how or when any of these dreams would become reality. Joseph had no idea that he would be sold as a slave into Egypt, that he would be elevated to positions of responsibility and then thrown unfairly into jail. He didn't know that he would be released from his imprisonment and would lead the great land of Egypt through times of prosperity and famine and that, through him, his own father and brothers would be saved from starvation. But throughout the written account of the story of Joseph, we find these words repeated: "The LORD was with Joseph and gave him success in whatever he did," or "The LORD was with Joseph and he prospered."

Those statements tell us that Joseph was not traveling this route alone. He was being led by the Lord and he was willingly following that direction even when obedience meant difficulty for him. Obedience does not always mean immediate rewards, but it does mean that our trust is in someone greater than ourselves.

Joseph was willing to obey one step at a time. Joseph never knew where the next step would take him, but when he sensed God's leading, he seemed to follow willingly, sometimes at great personal cost. The result of his obedience was a focused life that resulted in survival and eventual prosperity not only for himself but also for his family.

God is trustworthy. We know that he has the power and the love to make decisions that will ultimately benefit us. We can rest in him and be assured that our obedience will eventually be rewarded by an approving heavenly Father.

TUESDAY

M e d i t a t i o n

"I concentrate on doing exactly what you say—I always have and always will."
(Psalm 119:112 *The Message*)

What a great testimony in this verse. Do we concentrate on doing exactly what God says? He wants us to do so. Maybe we cannot say that we always have, but let's together make the commitment now to say that we always will!

Meditate on this verse and ask God to empower you to learn what he says and to follow his direction. Write your thoughts below.

J o u r n a l

WEDNESDAY

T h o u g h t s   f o r   t o d a y :

Joseph was a powerful earthly leader by the time he was a mature adult. Yet, he was humbly submissive to God's direction in his life. We, too, have to be willing to humble ourselves under God's leadership. If he wants a job done and asks one of us to do it, we must humbly accept the assignment and do it with all our might no matter what it is.

It also takes trusting submission to be willing to take the first step without knowing what the second and third steps will be. We like to be in on the plan. When we have humble spirits, we will commit to God and obey him even if he hasn't taken us into his confidence to share what the outcome of our obedience will be.

A simplified life of obedience to our heavenly Father has to begin deep within us. The Bible teaches that if we set our hearts on the things of God, obedience will come naturally. What if your heart is not quite that willing? What if you are not sure you can trust God quite that much? What if you have items on your own agenda that would be too hard to part with? How do you change the very desires of your heart?

T H U R S D A Y

Thoughts   for   today:

The pathway to a changed heart runs straight through the brain. We can control our thoughts. While we may not be able to keep thoughts from entering our minds, we can decide what thoughts will be allowed to stay. We are not helpless in nurturing our own spiritual growth, because our minds, which are under our control, are where a transformed life begins. If we carefully guard what information and images we take in, if we quickly rid ourselves of negative or sinful thoughts, and if we learn to focus our minds on God, his word, and his kingdom values, we will begin to change.

We need to walk with him, take our anxieties to him, listen for his voice, and eagerly learn to know his word. We need to pray daily and ask for his instructions for that day. We should not be afraid to ask the "What do you want me to do?" question because we know that he will not ask us to do anything that is not good for us, nor will he ask us to do anything that we, by his power and grace, are not able to accomplish. Once we adopt this attitude of submission, we begin to hear what he asks us to do and eventually it becomes the most natural thing in the world for us to obey.

F R I D A Y

Reading   God's   message

Genesis 39

Read this chapter from the life of Joseph. Do you begin to understand how committed Joseph was to doing the right thing? Do you see the consequences he was willing to suffer in order to stay true to his commitment to God? Now look at Verse 23 and realize that God honors those who are willing to put him first in their lives even when we don't know what the future may hold.

Journal

SATURDAY

For personal reflection

Think about what your life would look like if you were totally committed to God.

How would your level of stress change?

How would your key relationships change?

How would your attitude toward others change?

Perhaps the main change in your life would be that you would be focused on walking moment by moment in communication with and submission to God. What is one step you can take today to help that focus to become stronger in your life?

_____

_____

SUNDAY

Prayer

O, Lord, my Lord, how majestic is your name in all the earth. Quiet the internal dialogue so I can concentrate on your love which is drawing me. I want to be loved unconditionally. Hold me, Jesus, and don't let me go. I ask in your precious name.

My prayer:

_____

_____

_____

_____

_____

A Change of Heart

P r i n c i p l e   # 5

God lavishly rewards a life of humble obedience.

Have you ever positioned yourself to receive a compliment or an honor? If you have set things up right, the compliment will come. But because you have continued the situation, doesn't the compliment have a kind of hollowness to it? Don't you find that it isn't nearly as satisfying as you thought it would be? There is a better way to experience a fulfilled life. First, we choose the road of humility and then, if there is honor to be given, it comes from the hand of God and not from our own maneuvering.

If we want God to reward and honor our lives, we may need to take a closer look at what humility is from God's perspective. I believe that humility is

- not having our eyes on ourselves, but on God.
- not thinking about ourselves and the impression we are making.
- not insisting on having our own way.
- having a willingness to learn and to be taught.
- having a willingness to put God first in our focus, the needs of others second, and our own perspective last.

As humble followers of God we must set aside our own agendas, our insistence on knowing outcomes, our demand to understand the reasons for what God is asking, and instead simply follow what he asks us to do.

True humility puts God first without regard to our personal circumstances and without worry about what others around us will think. If we do that we are not focused on rewards, but God has some pretty nice surprise gifts waiting for those who honor him.

God desires that your life not only be uncluttered and simplified, but also that it be rich, rewarded, happy, and fulfilled. The Bible tells us that the rewards for obedience are great. Not only will God give us freedom from life's complexities and burdens if we obey him, but he has promised blessing besides. James 1:25 reads, "But the man who looks intently into the perfect law that gives freedom, and continues to do this, not forgetting what he has heard, but doing it—he will be blessed in what he does." Don't we all want to receive God's gracious gifts? His word gives us many promises related to obedience—including life, prosperity, recognition, sense of belonging, God's love, God's fellowship, answered prayers, wisdom, and understanding—if we are willing to be humbly obedient to his direction.

TUESDAY

Meditation

"Take on an entirely new way of life—a God-fashioned life, a life renewed from the inside and working itself into your conduct as God accurately reproduces his character in you."
(Ephesians 4:24, *The Message*)

Meditate on this command. Ask God to fashion your life as he wishes. Submit to the renewing work of the Holy Spirit in your inner being. Thank God for caring enough to shape your life into his perfect plan.

Journal

WEDNESDAY

Thoughts for today:

Here is a biblical listing of some of the rewards that come from a life of obedience to God:

Life and prosperity. "Walk in all the way that the Lord your God has commanded you, so that you may live and prosper..." (Deuteronomy 5:33). God's definition of prosperity and ours might differ, but I have learned that I am better off accepting his definition any day.

Recognition. "Whoever practices and teaches these commands will be called great in the kingdom of heaven." (Matthew 5:19). We are often looking for approval in all the wrong places. God says that if we obey him, he will make us great in his kingdom. Whose approval and recognition is most important?

A sense of belonging. "Whoever does the will of my Father in heaven is my brother and sister and mother." (Matthew 12:50). Sometimes we spend a great deal of effort in trying to fit in or to belong to a certain group. Only God offers a sense of true and total belonging.

God's love. "Whoever has my commands and obeys them, he is the one who loves me. He who loves me will be loved by my Father, and I too will love him..." (John 14:21). We realize at the depth of our being that being loved by God brings gives us a security that we can find in no other relationship.

THURSDAY

Thoughts for today:

Here are more promises we can claim if we are submissive to God's direction in our lives:

Answered prayers. "...we have confidence before God and receive from him anything we ask because we obey his commands and do what pleases him." (I John 3:21-22). The precedent to answered prayer is obedience because God says he longs to give good gifts to those who please him.

Wisdom and understanding. "The fear of the Lord is the beginning of wisdom; all who follow his precepts have good understanding..." (Psalm 111:10 NIV). True wisdom comes from knowing and doing the will of God. Our eyes are opened to spiritual things, to relationships, and to service when we humbly obey the God who reveals his direction to us.

The rewards for following God are the qualities that make life satisfying, joyful, purposeful. So, what holds us back from simple obedience?

- Lack of trust in the God who loves us more than we can know?
- Pride that is not willing to obey because we will lose control of our lives and may, in fact, look foolish?
- Failure to recognize God's leading?

The cure for all of these obedience-blockers is uncluttering our lives to the point where we can spend time with God, adjust our thoughts to his, hear his voice, and then be willing to respond when he asks us to obey.

FRIDAY

Reading God's message

Matthew 5:1–19

Jesus told us that he is the exact representation of God, his Father. Therefore, we need to pay close attention to what he taught when he came to this earth.

Read Jesus' teaching in this passage. What are the kinds of attitudes for which he promises blessing in the first 10 verses? How should we react when people don't understand us and persecute us? What do you think it means to be salt and light in this world? Why should we want people to see our good deeds? For what kind of behavior does Jesus promise greatness in his kingdom?

Journal

S A T U R D A Y

For personal reflection

Review the rewards outlined in this lesson.

Does God ever fail to make good on a promise? Then claim these promises as you live a life of obedience.

Which of these rewards would bring the greatest joy to your life today?

_____

Which of these rewards are you experiencing already?

_____

Commit to God to focus on him, to listen for his voice, and to follow wherever he leads. Then begin to watch as he blesses you with the promised rewards. He loves to give good gifts to his children!

S U N D A Y

Prayer

I want to be like you, Jesus. I want to know you better because I know how much I need you. Help me to wait on you and to follow you more closely. In your powerful name, Jesus. Amen.

My prayer:

_____

_____

_____

_____

_____

Rewards of Simple Obedience

P r i n c i p l e   # 6

Once we stop running from truth and turn instead to seek it, it will be found.

Who can argue with truth as a value to be pursued? We all agree, at least intellectually, that it is a good thing. But do you realize how much of the time in our lives we spend in running from or denying the truth?

Think about it. Women put on makeup in the morning to hide the truth of the face that we woke up with. We dress our bodies in clothing that is carefully chosen to be flattering to our shape and our coloring—in other words, to cover the truth of the flaws in our bodies. Many of us use deodorizing mouthwashes and underarm gels to mask the true odors we produce.

We may then go down to the kitchen and pour a bowl of flake cereal with "wild blueberries." True? Does the cereal maker actually go out into the meadows to pick "wild" berries to put in each box of cereal? While we eat, we turn on the television to find out if another war started last night while we slept. We notice that a story on Channel 3 has just a different slant to it than the same story on another network. Which is true?

But the advertisements, we can be sure, are presenting 100 percent truth. After all, they are very convincing! A certain brand of toothpaste will bring adoring admirers into our lives; and one insurance company can insure us when no one else will, while a new real estate company will sell houses that no other company can.

By the time you get to work, you are not sure if you can trust that the orange-capped coffee pot really holds the decaf. Who or what can you believe anymore? We are not stupid. We know we are being deceived on a daily, even hourly, basis. Yet we take it. We do not demand truth. Why? Maybe we are actually more comfortable in a life of lies, half-truths, and shaded facts. If we were not, wouldn't we protest being manipulated so blatantly?

Let's desire instead to discard the lies and half-truths that we may have accepted and move freely in the wide, wide fields of open honesty and truthful living. Then we will begin to experience what Jesus promised his followers, "…you will know the truth, and the truth will set you free." (John 8:32).

TUESDAY

Meditation

Meditate on the following verse from David's well known prayer of confession after he acknowledged tragic sin in his life. What does truth mean to you? What does it mean to God? What kind of "new, true life" might God be offering to you today?

"What you're after is truth from the inside out. Enter me, then; conceive a new, true life."
(Psalm 51:6 *The Message*)

Journal

WEDNESDAY

Thoughts for today:

As Christians, we are to be seekers of truth. Jesus defined himself as truth. If we are his followers, we are, by definition, followers of the truth. That truth, remember, will make us free.

- Free from being controlled by others.
- Free from our own prejudices and fears.
- Free from carrying guilt for sins forgiven.
- Free from having to be perfect.
- Free from our insecurities and doubts.

Most of all, truth will make us free to build our lives on a valid foundation. Without even being aware of it, some of us live our lives based on our acceptance as truth of some negative message that we were told as children:

- You're a slob.
- You'll never amount to anything.
- You have a big mouth.
- You're just like your father.
- You can't get along with anybody.

It is a growth process to sort through the messages of our lives and to discover which are true and which are lies. Once we have done that hard work, we can make decisions that are based on the truth of who we are and what we believe instead of on lies we have been told and have accepted as true.

THURSDAY

T h o u g h t s   f o r   t o d a y :

As children, we had no way of separating truth from falsehoods, so our little psyches accepted everything that an authority figure said to us as truth. Now that we are adults, we may intellectually be able to sort truth from lies in what we have been told, but our inner-self often accepts these false messages as valid, and those beliefs drive the decisions we make. By the time we reach mid-life, we may realize that choices we have made all along—who we married, the career path we chose, the home we live in, and even how we dress—were made based on falsehoods perpetrated early in our childhoods when we were vulnerable to receiving and accepting lies as truth.

Do you want to know truth? Would you like to be free from lies you have accepted about who you are? Are you ready to discard the untruths around us? There is a better way. You can choose the way of freedom. Jesus declared, "I am the way and the truth and the life." (John 14:6). Truth will be found in our relationship with Jesus, in knowledge of his word, and in the teaching that we receive from others who are related to him, too, and who are fellow truth-seekers in the journey of life.

FRIDAY

R e a d i n g   G o d ' s   m e s s a g e

John 8:31–47

Read this passage to determine how Jesus differentiates between truth and lies. Do you think that the religious leaders participating in this conversation really wanted to hear the truth? Do you want to know God's truth in your life? According to Verses 31 and 32, how can we know truth?

J o u r n a l

SATURDAY

For   personal   reflection

Ask God if there is a person in your life from whom you have been hiding the truth. If an individual comes to your mind, write down the following:

Name of the person from whom you have hidden the truth.

_____

The lie that you have allowed them to believe.

_____

The truth that must be told.

_____

Ask God for guidance and then begin to look for an opportunity to speak to that person from your heart, keeping in mind that the truth brought into the light will bring healing and freedom.

SUNDAY

Prayer

Lord Jesus, at times when I am afraid, I will trust in you. You never let me down and your word is true and will hold me up. Thank you for these tools of life—your word and my prayers. I bless your name, Jesus.

My prayer:

_____

_____

_____

_____

_____

Looking for the Truth

Principle   #7

When we think we have discovered truth, we need to look one layer deeper to see if what we've found is truth from God or a lie from man.

J. Keith Miller in his recent book, *The Secret Life of the Soul,* discusses the frustration experienced by many Christians who commit their lives to Christ and then do not undergo any long-lasting change. Their behavior might be modified for awhile, but soon they fall into old patterns and find themselves going back again and again for recommitment or spiritual renewal. The book is a psychological study of what Miller calls "constructed personalities."

He says that we learn early in our life which behaviors and feelings are acceptable and which are not. Then we each begin to construct a personality that is acceptable within the society in which we find ourselves. As a result, each of us has constructed a personality that we show to the outside world and that we come to believe is our true self but, in reality, is a false self, constructed in response to negative or false messages we have received. When we commit our lives to Christ, then, we commit this constructed self to him and our real personalities remain buried and hidden under years of false living.

Miller says, "We are, in effect, asking God to bless our unreal lives, our manipulative and non-trusting means of getting self esteem.... Remember, the soul seeks and demands a spiritual, or real, connection with God, with people, with ourselves and our motives, and with vocational choices...a constructed person cannot have the intimate and spiritual relationship with God that the soul cries out for because the constructed personality is not real. Spiritually, reality and unreality evidently cannot mix" (Broadman & Holman Publishers, 1997, p. 131).

It was a revelation to me to realize that I needed to know my real self before I could relate intimately with God. But it makes sense, doesn't it? If I did not understand who I was, I could only offer him who I thought I was. I didn't know, until God began to reveal truth through counseling, through reading good authors, and through the study of his word, who I really was. This is a process that takes a lifetime. But it is worth the effort to peel back layer after layer of the constructed personality and to find out who God really created us to be before we began to get buried in false messages about who we are or who we should be in order to be accepted by people.

T U E S D A Y

M e d i t a t i o n

Read the following verses and meditate on what God's message might be to you from this passage:

"Investigate my life, O God, find out everything about me;
Cross-examine and test me, get a clear picture of what I'm about;
See for yourself whether I've done anything wrong—then guide me on the road to eternal life."
(Psalm 139:23–24 *The Message*)

J o u r n a l

W E D N E S D A Y

T h o u g h t s   f o r   t o d a y :

Jesus says that he is the truth. There is only one reality and it is found in him. In order to get to a true and honest relationship with him, we have to dig through all the clutter that we have allowed to complicate and confuse our lives because we have not heard and assimilated simple truth.

First, we have to be willing to face the truth about ourselves. Who are we really? We know that we are not the image we project to others. But are we the person we have allowed ourselves to believe we are? God, through the light of his word and through the promptings of the Holy Spirit within you, can reveal truth to us if we are willing and receptive. However, if we have any sense that truth about ourselves may be locked inside barriers of untruths told and accepted throughout our lifetimes, it may be of great benefit to seek a professional counselor who is first of all committed to God and then trained in psychological principles. This trained guide can help us reach our innermost beings and know and understand ourselves as we truly are.

Once we reach that goal, the truth of God and of his word can break through to our real selves. At that point healing and growth can begin!

T H U R S D A Y

T h o u g h t s   f o r   t o d a y :

In our efforts to reach our true selves, we probably will find that we have complicated our personalities far beyond what God intended. Our needs and our desires are simple and universal. We are simple beings needing only to connect to God and to one another. That's really all there is to it!

Truth is evidenced by that kind of simplicity. It is often found in the "Aha" experiences of life—all of a sudden, after we have spent hours in discussion, and in reading and research, a solution appears that was there all along, but we failed to recognize it.

The simplicity of truth is found only in accepting that the kind of "Aha" understanding we want can sometimes be realized only after we have waded through lots of evidence, stretched our minds, and then fallen back to what we knew but had not recognized or acknowledged.

The promise of being able to find that truth is held out to us by Christ when he invites us to follow him; and it is his promise that keeps us digging, even when the going gets tough, to find the real truth about who we are and about what matters in life. This is the kind of truth that is God-sent. It is the kind of truth that sets us free!

F R I D A Y

R e a d i n g   G o d ' s   m e s s a g e

I Timothy 1:1–7

Read carefully this passage and note how it points to Jesus as the giver of truth and the one who frees us from our captivity to sin and lies. What does Paul say is the work he has been called to do in relationship to this truth? Do we have the same commission? What do you think God wants you to do to get his message out to others who do not know the truth he reveals?

J o u r n a l

SATURDAY

For personal reflection

Think about what others have told you about yourself throughout your life. Which of those messages are from God and which are lies that you have accepted as truth?

_____

_____

Ask God to reveal to you the truth of who you are in him. Allow the realization of his love for you to penetrate your very soul.

_____

_____

Then love him back, thanking him for the light of the truth that he gives.

SUNDAY

Prayer

Holy Spirit, you are the spirit of truth and will guide me into all truth. Help me, remind me, alert me to ask for your guidance and gladly follow it. I adore you, soul of my soul.

My prayer:

_____

_____

_____

_____

_____

Seeing the Simple Truth

P r i n c i p l e   # 8

Truth revealed is truth revered.

Knowing truth is very often more of a recognition or a realization than it is a discovery. That is why people can study all their lives in the best of educational institutions and miss the real truths of life. Finding truth is not a result of research, it is a gift that God gives to those who seek him. Remember, Jesus and truth are synonymous.

We don't get to know Jesus better (and thus truth) just by studying. We get to know him as a result of his willingness to reveal himself to us as we spend time with him. Certainly this will involve study and reading of his word as we will discuss below, but revelation is obtained through relationship more than in any other way.

If we examine John 8:32 and read it in *The Message*, we find that it says, "… you will experience for yourselves the truth, and the truth will free you." This translation opens up for us the concept that truth is an experience—not just a body of knowledge.

When a mother has her first child, she spends time reading baby books, making sure she knows everything she needs to know about caring for her new baby: what to feed him, how to burp him, what safety concerns she should have, and so on. She can read volume after volume on child care, but the fact of the matter is that she gets to know the child by revelation as she spends time with him. No one will know better how to calm a crying baby than his mother. Why? She knows him best. She has observed his behaviors. She understands his needs and his comforts. Has he verbalized those things? No. Has he sent her a letter explaining his wants, needs, and infant language? No, but he has revealed them and the truth about her son is known to her because she has learned to discern those revelations.

The same is true in our relationship to God, the giver of all truth. In John 14:16–17, Jesus says, "And I will ask the Father, and he will give you another Counselor to be with you forever—the Spirit of truth." This Spirit indwells those of us who are followers of Christ and has promised to reveal the truth about God, about ourselves, about good and evil, about other people, and about the world systems around us. We just have to become receivers of those revelations.

TUESDAY

Meditation

**"I'm ecstatic over what you say, like one who strikes it rich.
I hate lies—can't stand them!—but I love what you have revealed... .
For those who love what you reveal, everything fits—no stumbling around
in the dark for them."**
(Psalm 119:163 and 165 *The Message*)

Read and meditate on these verses. Then thank God for the revelation he is
willing to give you. What is he trying to reveal to you through the words of
this passage on which you are meditating today?

Journal

WEDNESDAY

Thoughts for today:

The primary avenue for receiving truth into our lives is through the Bible.
The psalmist says to God in Psalm 119:160, "All your words are true." Jesus,
in praying to the Father in John 17:17 says, "Sanctify them by the truth; your
word is truth." Do you believe that the Bible is true? Do you believe that it
reveals God? That it reveals the real you? If so, you can approach your reading of God's word with an attitude of finding the plain, life-changing truth
that you seek.

Begin your search by asking the Holy Spirit to enlighten you as you read
and study so that your eyes will behold truth and so that you will see clearly
where you may have been misled into accepting untruth or partial truth as
God's truth. Accept the correction of those deceptions that you have lived out
in your life. Remember, you have access to the spirit of truth. When you are
willing to see truth, he is willing to reveal it!

You can trust that God not only will give you answers and revelations that
are perfect in their truthfulness, but be assured that he is standing by, just
waiting for you to ask. If you have faith enough to ask, he has love enough to
answer.

THURSDAY

Thoughts for today:

We need to be diligent in reading and studying the word of God for ourselves, allowing the Holy Spirit to teach us. Remember that Bible teachers and pastors are human beings and they filter God's truth through their own lenses. We should listen to what they say and then dig into the Bible to verify its application to our lives.

There is one other caution: Satan is the great counterfeiter and, in Jesus' own words in John 8:44, "...When he lies, he speaks his native language, for he is a liar and the father of lies." The way we can see through Satan's lies is to be connected to the truth of the Bible and to be walking in the light of relationship with Christ. When we do those things, we become discerners of truth through the revelation of Christ and the Holy Spirit.

We have become accustomed to living in a world of half-truths and outright lies. Doesn't that tell you who has control of the world right now? Satan, the father of lies, loves using the diluted and twisted truth to manipulate our lives. He loves creating doubts about the goodness of God and his work on our behalf. Our relationship with Jesus and our understanding of his word will set us free from that manipulation as we see through the lies we are told and, instead, recognize truth.

FRIDAY

Reading God's message

Matthew 11:25–30

What does this passage tell us about the kind of people to whom God reveals his truth? What reason does Jesus give us for God choosing to do this? How can we know God the Father better, according to these verses? In what ways has Jesus been revealed to us? What do you think is the role of revelation in understanding God's truth? What is the role of Scripture? What is the role of knowing Christ's life and teaching? Are you taking advantages of all of these ways to know truth?

Journal

SATURDAY

For personal reflection

As you go through your life today, be aware of the indwelling Holy Spirit, and breathe prayers to him, asking that he will let you see the people around you as he sees them.

Ask him to reveal the truth of the needs of people's hearts, of the motivations of their actions, and of the pitfalls that they might present to your spiritual life.

Respond to them according to the truth that God reveals.

_____

_____

_____

_____

SUNDAY

Prayer

Father, thank you for giving me your word just when I need it. It is more than words, it is a force, a power that lifts the veil to see you and experience your loving presence. Stay with me, Jesus. I ask in your name. Amen.

My prayer:

_____

_____

_____

_____

_____

Truth Revealed by God's Spirit

P r i n c i p l e   # 9

God's truth is a mystery revealed and a power released.

Believing the things that God says about us can set us on a pathway to truth that will encourage our hearts to understand all that he has in mind for us in this life and the life to come. But God will not reveal everything. There are some things he reserves as mysteries to be uncovered when we see him face to face.

When we get a little bit of truth, we want more. That is a healthy appetite and one that we should constantly feed. But we should not be frustrated by what we do not yet know. Even Paul had the experience of partial understanding. As we read through Romans, Chapters 9 through 11, Paul goes back and forth on the issue of God's election and sovereign choices over our lives versus the free will of human beings. He gives all his arguments in an effort to make the issue as clear as possible for his readers. But at the end of all of the teaching, he seems to pause and take a deep breath, concluding his dissertation with these words: "Oh, the depth of the riches of the wisdom and knowledge of God! How unsearchable his judgments, and his paths beyond tracing out!"

I heard an astronomer speak recently. He was highly educated and had many years of experience in studying the cosmos, stars, black holes, nebulae, galaxies, solar systems, and the expanding universe. When asked how he, as a Christian, dealt with the issue of creation, he responded simply, yet profoundly. He said that God was the designer and creator of the universe. How he did it, according to this scientist, is "details." To illustrate, he told about a t-shirt message he saw which began with, "And God said 'Let there be light.'" Then there was a series of complex formulae written out on the shirt, concluding with, "And there was light." This astronomer could have given a complicated answer because he possessed a vast wealth of knowledge of this universe. But his answer, simple in its truth, acknowledged the sovereignty of our creator, but allowed the mystery of God's creative methods to remain unknown and to be accepted in simple faith.

As we grow closer to God, we learn to know that he is trustworthy and, therefore, we can treasure and apply the things that we do know and trust him with what we cannot yet understand.

TUESDAY

Meditation

"We don't yet see things clearly. We're squinting in a fog, peering through a mist. But it won't be long before the weather clears and the sun shines bright! We'll see it all then, see it all as clearly as God sees us, knowing him directly just as he knows us!"
(I Corinthians 13:12 *The Message*)

What does this passage say to you? Meditate especially on the last phrase and contemplate what it will be like to know God as thoroughly as he knows us now.

Journal

WEDNESDAY

Thoughts for today:

As we grow in our knowledge of God, we become more aware of his vastness and of the futility in thinking we can know him fully, at least while we are in our earthly life. As time goes on, I have become more and more accepting of mystery and, in faith, believe that God will reveal the truth that I need to know, the truth that he wants me to know, and the truth that he knows I am ready to accept and apply. He doesn't seem to want to waste revealed truth if I am not ready to receive it and put it to use in my life. And it seems that he wants to hold some things back from us to have surprises to reveal in the life to come. We will be ready for it then!

As Christ followers, we have access to truth that nonbelievers do not have. We don't have to stumble around in the world of the intellect and of human-contrived philosophies. We can enter the world of the learned with insight given by God himself and with the truth that we know from his word. We have access into the presence of the one who is truth personified. This connection gives our lives meaning and depth and purpose unknown to those who do not know God.

THURSDAY

Thoughts for today:

Leslie Vernick, in her book *How to Live Right When Your Life Goes Wrong*, points out that if we are to reach our full potential as human beings, we have to "enter into another dimension of reality that is not common to human experience" (Waterbrook Press, 2003, p. 113). That dimension of reality is truth, real truth, not as the world and Satan have distorted it, but the reality of God's truth, his plan, his desires for us, and the living out of our lives in a way that is consistent with God's reality.

Once we know that truth, our response to it must be immediate. We cannot see truth and then decide whether or not we will believe it, accept it, or obey it. Truth and response go together. It's a package deal.

In order for us to live lives that are

- productive and not just busy,
- effective and not just successful,
- nurturing and not just functional, and
- spiritual at a level of ever-growing relationship with God,

we must build those lives on a foundation of truth. That means discovering truth in every area of our lives, including emotional, relational, and spiritual. Our sources for truth are the study of the Bible, listening to the revelation of the Holy Spirit, walking in fellowship with Jesus, and entering into honest relationships with other believers who are also truth seekers.

FRIDAY

Reading God's message

Ephesians 1:3–23

Read this passage carefully, paying particular attention to Verses 17–19. Who or what is the source of our understanding and truth, according to these verses? How do we access that knowledge? What is the result of knowing God's truth?

Journal

SATURDAY

For   personal   reflection

Spend some time in thinking of the greatness of God, his majesty, his power, his wisdom, and his eternal nature.

Write down words or phrases that come to your mind as you try to describe the greatness of God.

_____

_____

_____

Enjoy what you know of him and look forward to someday knowing that which now is hidden in mystery.

Pray, thanking God for revealing himself and his truth and for promising to show you more and more as you walk day-by-day with him.

SUNDAY

Prayer

My Father, I want more of your surprising light because in your light I see light. I can tell that you are enjoying every moment with me. Help me carve out more moments to spend together with you.

My prayer:

_____

_____

_____

_____

_____

The Mystery and Power of Truth

P r i n c i p l e   # 10

**The goal of my soul
Is to cling to my King!**

Over the past few weeks, we have talked about truth. In that process, you may have discovered some things about yourself that you don't like. Maybe there are some things that you would like to change. As humans, our first reaction is to get busy—after all, God expects us to do our best. Maybe you decide to head to the store, buy one of the many self-improvement books on the shelves, and go to work on yourself. I am suggesting that you resist that temptation. Instead, stop to take a look at the areas for growth that you have identified in your life. Do you have a desire for

- more purpose?
- more significance?
- more purity?
- greater understanding?
- more direction from God?
- more focus on that which is of real value?
- greater spiritual sensitivity?

If you have discovered any of these desires in your heart, don't ignore them. That discovery is God's invitation

- to grow in effectiveness,
- to develop into all that he means for you to be, and
- to draw closer in relationship to him.

The keys to personal growth provided for reflection through this week will help us to stop doing what is natural for us to do as human beings when we sense a need: to try harder. Instead, we will find ourselves turned toward the only one who can work a transformation within us and surprise us with the result!

The effectiveness of our lives for God's kingdom will be a direct reflection of the degree of our willingness to cling to him. If we turn our attention toward relating to God and turn our minds away from our often failed self-improvement plans, we will be connected to the source of our true growth and our only real means of making purposeful change in our lives. The change God brings about is a change from the inside out. It is supernatural; it is not the result of our efforts. All he asks of us is that we stay close to him. He will produce the results that he wants in our lives.

The personal and spiritual growth we desire will come about by refusing to focus on our own need for transformation and by detaching from all the self-improvement methods that have failed so completely in the past and, instead, clinging to our source of life and hope and light—to God himself.

TUESDAY

Meditation

Read and meditate on this verse of instruction that Jesus gave to his disciples just before he was arrested and killed. Let God reveal to you what he means by living in him, by making our home in him, and by being joined to him.

"Live in me. Make your home in me just as I do in you. In the same way that a branch can't bear grapes by itself but only by being joined to the vine, you can't bear fruit unless you are joined to me."
(John 15:4 *The Message*)

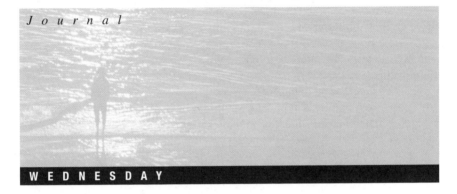

Journal

WEDNESDAY

Thoughts for today:

When we attach to God, we are free from the efforts, the worry, and the anxieties associated with change, and we simply enjoy the intimacy of relationship with him. He does all the rest. Paul tells God's followers not to worry about anything, but instead to pray about everything (Philippians 4:6). The result, he promises, is that God will flood their hearts with peace that is beyond human understanding. From anxiety to peace. From self-focus to God-focus. That is transformation. That is God-centered living. That is what we all want as we long for personal growth and meaningful relationship with our heavenly Father.

Pause for a moment and think about what you focus on during any given day. Is it the problems you face? Is it the goals you have set? Is it the crisis immediately in front of you? Is it a desire to grow spiritually? As we think about commitment during these next few days, I would challenge you with this statement: It's not about you, it's about *him*. By being willing to commit 100 percent to God, we take our eyes off ourselves, our problems, our relationships, and, yes, even our spiritual growth, and put them totally and solely on our heavenly father. When our attention is on the God we serve, everything changes; but we are neither the agents nor the focus of that change.

THURSDAY

Thoughts for today:

The essential secret of spiritual growth is this: You cannot change, but you can be changed! You don't have to change yourself. You only have to focus on God and give him permission to make the changes he wants to make in his own way and in his own time.

Jesus gave his disciples an illustration of a vine and its branches. The branches cannot urge themselves to grow grapes, nor can they prune themselves to become more fruitful. They simply hang onto the vine from which they obtain all life-giving resources. When the vine and the branches are well connected, fruit begins to develop and then to grow and to become all that the master gardener intended. Jesus is our vine. We are to stay connected to him as we go through the moments, hours, days, weeks, and years of our lives.

What does it take to be able to continue in such connectedness? We, as human beings, will naturally cling to that which we trust. Therefore, the key to relationship with God is to trust him.

- Trust that he loves you.
- Trust that he will be true to all that he has promised in the Bible.
- Trust that the changes he makes in you and in your life will be for your benefit and will enable you to become all that he has in mind for you to be: filled with joy, purpose, meaning, and satisfaction.

FRIDAY

Reading God's message

Psalm 62

Read this passage and think about these questions: What does this psalm teach us about God? What do we learn about David's desire for relationship with God? What advice does David give to the people of Israel? What comforting characteristics of God does he point out in the last two verses of the psalm?

Journal

SATURDAY

For personal reflection

Do you feel drawn to God? If so, it is because he is inviting you into closer, more intimate relationship with him.

Respond to his call by
- turning to him,
- focusing on him, and
- allowing him to work change in your life over a period of time as you stay connected through prayer, Bible reading, and association with other Christians.

Write down specific things that you can do on a daily or weekly basis to connect to God in the ways listed above.

_____

_____

_____

SUNDAY

Prayer

Come, Holy Spirit, keep this unbroken companionship with you moving forward. Thank you for your assurance that I can never be separated from love. Help me believe it, Lord Jesus. In your powerful name I ask. Amen.

My prayer:

_____

_____

_____

_____

_____

Just Keep Hanging On

P r i n c i p l e   # 11

True life that is fresh and free and full is found only in undistracted connection to God.

Each of us has some area of our lives with which we are not satisfied. And as we think of that problem area, we begin to berate ourselves for not being better, for not measuring up, and for not being able to get on top of the situation and do better. Think about your life. What are some areas about which you are self-critical?

Do you think

- you should you be spending more time with your children?
- you should be more disciplined in your spending?
- you should you do a better job of keeping up the house and yard?
- you should be more dedicated to your work?
- you should take better care of your health by exercising and eating better?
- you should be less critical of your spouse?
- you should be more patient with your neighbor or co-worker?
- you should be spending more time in Bible reading and prayer?
- you should go to church more regularly and get more involved?

We spend a lot of emotional energy in self-criticism, worry, guilt, and despair about situations we may have no power to change. We really want to change and we are willing to go through lots of self-discipline to get there. After all, we have been told that God helps those who help themselves. But, after repeated failures, we begin to feel pretty helpless. It's OK to give up. In fact, today is the day we are going to stop doing what doesn't work. Instead, we must rechannel that negative energy to a productive end. Remember, it's not about us—it's about God. If we are worried or carrying guilt about any (or all) of the things mentioned above, we have the wrong focus! The focus needs to be turned to God and away from ourselves!

Giving up the struggle is sometimes the most difficult part of the growing process, but just for today, let's agree to stop trying to solve all our personal problems, stop trying to improve ourselves, and, instead, simply commit ourselves and our lives to God. We have failed miserably at all the self-improvement programs we have adopted anyway. What do we have to lose by giving up? Let's turn to God because we need him, because he is waiting for us to come to him, and because he is truly our only hope of becoming any better than we are today.

TUESDAY

Meditation

Read the following verses slowly; then go back to a phrase that speaks to you. Meditate on it for a few minutes, asking God to reveal to you what he wants you to know or experience from his word today. Ask him to make these words real to you, just as if you had written them yourself.

"God—you're my God! I can't get enough of you! I've worked up such hunger and thirst for God, traveling across dry and weary deserts. So here I am in the place of worship, eyes open, drinking in your strength and glory. In your generous love I am really living at last!"
(Psalm 63:1–3 *The Message*).

Journal

WEDNESDAY

Thoughts for today:

Our own sense of insecurity, inadequacy, and inferiority are the three "i's" that keep us focused on ourselves. Do you relate to any of those three words? We don't get rid of the three "i's" by trying harder. In fact, these particular feelings seem to thrive on the attention we give them and grow even stronger and more tenacious by our efforts.

We get rid of them by starving them, by not paying attention to them, and instead by giving all of our attention to God. It's a simple idea, but it is not easy to do. Our egos are powerful and drive us to think that we can overcome these obstacles by ourselves.

Amazing things will begin to happen in our lives if we persist in our commitment to God instead of persisting in trying harder.

Over time, we find that
- we will be free of our past,
- we will be free of self-consciousness,
- we will be free of sins that have a stronghold on us, and
- we will be free to serve God, to grow up in him, and to become the strong, fulfilled, men and women that he has planned for us to be.

And over time we will find that the insecurities, inadequacies, and feelings of inferiority will no longer be getting our attention and they will have lost the power to control our lives.

THURSDAY

Thoughts   for   today:

We now know that our struggle and our efforts in self-improvement are ineffective in bringing about permanent change. Change in us comes about only by the supernatural and loving intervention of God himself. When we begin to learn to cling to him and to focus solely on our relationship with him,

- we will care much less what we look like and, in fact,
- our wrinkles begin to become attractive to those around us,
- our eating will begin to be under control and our weight will become what it should be,
- our worries will seem less important and will no longer cause us distracting anxiety,
- our work will take its proper place in our hierarchy of time use,
- our critical spirit toward others around us will lessen,
- our devotional life will grow out of our focus on God and will not become just one more "task" that demands our attention and causes us guilt.

We will begin to take great pleasure in pleasing God and will focus less and less on pleasing ourselves. The rewards of the heavenward focus are experienced, not only in the life to come, but also in our day-to-day living here on earth. These rewards are worth the effort and the time it takes to cling to our Father in heaven.

FRIDAY

Reading   God's   message

Galatians 5

Read this chapter thoughtfully. What does Paul point out as the only thing that matters (V. 6)? What does he say in Verse 13 about how we should relate to one another? What solution to sinful desires does he give in verse 16? What fruit will grow in our lives if we remain connected to the Spirit of God (VV. 22-23)?

Journal

SATURDAY

For personal reflection

Are you dissatisfied or preoccupied with an area of your life? Write it here:

_____

_____

_____

Commit today to stop focusing on that area. When the problem comes to your mind, turn it over to God in prayer and tell him that you yield to his will in changing the circumstances if he so desires or in changing you if that is his plan.

You, instead of worrying and planning, will stay committed and connected to him and will allow him to take over the area of your life which has become too big a focus. Let God have your attention instead of directing it to your problem.

SUNDAY

Prayer

Father, I know that I have the choice to make—to trust or to be afraid—because I can't do both. In your truth, Holy Spirit, I will find the freedom to be a non-anxious presence in my world. Your will be done in Jesus' name. Amen.

My prayer:

_____

_____

_____

_____

_____

Look Up, Not In

P r i n c i p l e   # 12

Turning toward God puts me face-to-face with him. He draws me closer one step at a time.

If you decided today that you are going to take a trip to see the Rocky Mountains, you would begin a process that would eventually get you there. I imagine you might start by looking on the Internet for information about the area, hotels you can stay in, tours and adventures you can sign up for. You would check with airlines to see what tickets cost and would decide if you are going to fly or drive. You would check schedules for yourself and consult with your traveling companions. Eventually plans are finalized, bookings are made, itineraries are set, and you anticipate the day when you will lay eyes on the Rockies.

When the day of the journey dawns, you have a choice to make. You can decide to sleep in (after all, you rationalize, you were up late last night packing). If you make that choice, however, you will miss the plane. So you may decide that, even though that soft pillow feels pretty good, you will get up, grab your luggage, and get yourself to the airport. If you don't take that important first step, you will not reach your destination.

What important first step is God asking you to take? Sometimes it is a simple matter of committing to spend more time reading and studying the Bible, or in praying more faithfully, or in listening for God's direction. At other times, the first step might be committing to give up a bad habit, changing jobs, redirecting financial resources, or renewing broken relationships. He will tell you what to do as you cling to him.

The first step we take in God's direction may seem small at the time, but if it turns us around and gets our focus on him, we cannot begin to measure its significance! God often tests our commitment to him by asking us to take a first step; that step will lead to another, and another, and another and, before we realize it, we are no longer looking at our feet—we are gazing into the face of our Lord and Savior and he is guiding our steps, one at a time.

Obedience by that time will have become almost automatic!

Just be willing to take whatever next step he may put in your path to growth, knowing that he will never ask you to do anything he has not prepared you to be able to do. Trust him to know what is best for you and take a step in obedience to his gentle leading.

TUESDAY

Meditation

"Trust God from the bottom of your heart; don't try to figure out everything on your own. Listen for God's voice in everything you do, everywhere you go; he's the one who will keep you on track."
(Proverbs 3:5–6 *The Message*)

Think about the message of these verses. Then meditate on one word or phrase that seems to touch your heart. Let God speak to you through His Word.

Journal

WEDNESDAY

Thoughts for today:

The book of Ruth in the Old Testament tells the story of a young woman who took an extreme first step when she left the teachings with which she was raised in order to follow the God of her husband's family. Years earlier, Naomi had journeyed with her husband and two sons from Judah to Moab at a time of famine in their homeland. While in Moab, the two sons married Moabite women, Ruth and Orpah. Then, all three of these women faced one of the most traumatic events any woman can face in her lifetime: Their husbands died.

Naomi had originally come from Judah and, now that her husband and sons were dead, she decided to return home to live among her own people. Ruth and Orpah were Moabite women and felt more at home among people they knew. They would more likely be able to find second husbands in their own land, so, when Naomi decided to return home, she encouraged Ruth and Orpah to remain in Moab. The decisions they made would set the course of their lives forever. Often we know that there is great impact in the decisions we face. At other times, a seemingly insignificant choice results in a dramatic change in our circumstances. At the core of every choice made by those who are God followers is commitment to him. With that basic decision made, all others will follow according to his perfect plan.

THURSDAY

Thoughts for today:

In the story of Ruth as told in the Bible, it seems that the two widowed sisters needed to renew their lives and put the sad memories associated with Naomi and their husbands out of their minds. In seeking to meet those needs, it seemed practical for them to remain in Moab while their mother-in-law, an Israelite, returned to her own country.

Orpah agreed with Naomi's direction to stay in Moab even though she seemed to have a sincere emotional attachment to her mother-in-law. Ruth, on the other hand, insisted upon going with Naomi. Her reasons for devotion to Naomi seem to be based on Ruth's faith in God. In Ruth 1:16, she says to Naomi, "Where you go I will go, and where you stay I will stay. Your people will be my people and your God my God."

It appears that Ruth had realized that Naomi's God was the one true God, and she wanted to follow her mother-in-law to the land where he was worshipped and where she could be obedient to him. In turning away from Moab and toward Israel, she was, in fact, turning away from focus on herself and her negative circumstances and focusing on God and his might instead. This turned out to be an important first step that made dramatic and eternal changes in Ruth's life.

FRIDAY

Reading God's message

Ruth 1

For the next few weeks, we will be looking at the book of Ruth and studying the committed life that Ruth lived with her God and with her family. Read the first chapter of this great story and think about the situation in which Ruth found herself and what she did to overcome her difficulties.

Journal

SATURDAY

For personal reflection

Is there a step in your life that God is asking you to take? If so, you already know what it is. Write it down.

_____

_____

_____

Now, don't let anything keep you from moving in God's direction. Don't be afraid to follow God's leading. He is looking out for you and knows what is best. That's where trust comes in.

Begin today to do whatever it is that he is asking you to do. He will honor your obedience and your commitment and you will begin to experience change in your life and growth in your spirit.

SUNDAY

Prayer

Lord, you tell me in your word that you are all I need, but my flesh cries out for more. I can't solve this, Lord. Help me to start over again. Quiet your child and just let me let you love me. I don't want to live a life of quiet desperation. Help!

My prayer:

_____

_____

_____

_____

_____

Taking the First Step

Principle # 13

**Just for today, choose to have an attitude of joy and hope.
Tomorrow, making that choice will be easier.**

While the three women in the story of Ruth are all experiencing similar circumstances, they all respond differently in terms of attitude. We can tell a lot about each of these women by the attitudes they chose. Orpah opted for the familiar and seemed to pull back from new ideas and adventure. Her focus seemed to be on her personal security and comfort. Naomi, on the other hand, focused on her negative feelings and became angry and resentful; she even changed her name to Mara, which means bitter. And whom does she blame for her trouble? God. She understood that God is the one in control but she did not seem to believe that he was acting out of love.

Then there was Ruth. I am sure she was just as overcome with grief as Orpah was, but she seemed to adopt two attitudes that the other women lacked: First she was concerned about Naomi in her grief; after all Naomi had lost not only a husband, but also two sons. Second, she was committed, as we previously pointed out, to the God of her husband and mother-in-law. In both cases, she was seeing beyond her own self. She was concerned about a suffering woman whom she loved, and she seemed to trust the God who had more control over the situation than she had.

Ruth and Naomi arrived in Bethlehem at the time of the barley harvest. In those days there were no food stamps or public assistance, so those who were poverty stricken were allowed to follow the harvesters of the grain crops and to pick up any grain that had fallen behind. Gleaning was not very fruitful, and it was hard work. Remember, this story took place in Israel where it is hot, dry, and sunny. Gleaning involved back-breaking bending and picking up the small amounts of leftover grain. Ruth could have considered herself too good to do this kind of menial labor; she could have decided she would wait for a better career move; she could have asked Naomi to go with her. But, she took this responsibility on herself without complaint.

Ruth did not wallow in self-pity for her own grief and her desperate situation. Instead, she chose to be a friend to Naomi, to take on responsibility for their sustenance, and to turn her eyes toward the one true God. Those were choices that God rewarded with his blessing.

TUESDAY

Meditation

"...fix your attention on God. You'll be changed from the inside out. Readily recognize what he wants from you and quickly respond to it. Unlike the culture around you, always dragging you down to its level of immaturity, God brings the best out of you, develops well-formed maturity in you."
(Romans 12:2b *The Message*)

Let the words of this verse sink deep into your heart as you meditate on their message. Carry the phrase, "fix your attention on God" with you as you go about your activities of this day.

Journal

WEDNESDAY

Thoughts for today:

When Boaz, the owner of the field where Ruth was working, asked about her, the foreman indicated that she had worked steadily all day (Ruth 2:7). Boaz was impressed. He called her aside and suggested that she glean in his field only. He also provided protection from the male harvesters who may have had an eye on her, and he allowed her to drink from his water jars when she was thirsty. She was touched by his kindness and asked why he would extend himself in this way for her since she was a foreigner. He responded that he had heard the story of her widowhood and, more importantly, of how kindly she had treated her mother-in-law (Ruth 2:11). By the third chapter of Ruth, the whole town knows the kind of person Ruth is.

Counselors tend to agree that this focus outside of self often is helpful in treating depression and insecurity. We have seen it happen over and over that when someone is serving another and involved in another's welfare, concern about self disappears. Ruth performed with grace and willingness the task that God had set before her. She did not ask for a road map to see where this path would lead; she simply was obedient to do what was at hand; and she did it with gusto! Remember, our spirituality is not about us, it is about God. Ruth had the right focus.

THURSDAY

Thoughts for today:

Ruth's can-do attitude and true character had become evident. Her conversation with Boaz convinced him that she was someone special. He offers her food and drink and arranges to have the harvesters drop extra grain so that, when Ruth gleaned, she obtained more food.

What struggles are we facing right now? Marriage conflicts, troubled adolescents, loneliness, fear, financial stresses, a frustrating job? Whatever our situations may be, we must be obedient to what is in front of us to do and continue in that action with an attitude of trust until God reveals the next step for us to take. If we are in a situation in which we truly do not know what to do next, we must pray, asking God to reveal the next step to take. Then, even if it seems difficult to do, we must take that step. Then we stay in that place until he moves us again.

The right attitude resulted in Ruth's being rewarded for her selflessness and her faithful service. What attitude does God want to change in us today? We can't change it by willpower. It won't work. Instead, we need to yield our negative thoughts and mindsets to God and ask him to replace our attitude with whatever he chooses so that we can cling even more closely to him and live out our lives in relationship to others in a way which he will reward.

FRIDAY

Reading God's message

Ruth 2

You may wish to review Ruth, Chapter 1, to remind yourself of Ruth's situation at the end of that chapter. Then read Chapter 2 and make note of the characteristics of Ruth that are revealed in her actions, in her speech, and in what others have been saying about her. What do you admire about her? In what ways does she serve as an example for us in our lives today?

Journal

SATURDAY

For personal reflection

Ask God to reveal any attitude in your heart that he wants to change.

Do you find that you are sometimes angry, bitter, untrusting, arrogant, vindictive, unforgiving, or unloving?

Stop justifying your right to feel that way you do and, instead, give up those negative feelings to God.

Write down any attitude that you feel God is asking you to submit to him.

_____

_____

Ask God to replace them with the attitudes he wants you to have: Love, joy, peace, patience, gentleness, humility, goodness, kindness, self-control, and thanksgiving.

SUNDAY

Prayer

Lord, you have given me power to choose my thoughts; thank you for this and give me the grace to make wise choices. I want your purity, Jesus. Put me on the path where this process will work new life in me one day at a time.

My prayer:

_____

_____

_____

_____

_____

Choosing Your Attitude

P r i n c i p l e # 14

What seems like a risk to me is no risk at all under the watchful and guiding eye of my heavenly Father.

When Ruth explained to Naomi how she had gathered so much grain in one day and went on to explain the kindnesses of Boaz, Naomi was impressed. As the harvests went on, Naomi began to be renewed in her relationship with God and began to grow closer and closer to Ruth, who had proved to be a faithful and loving daughter-in-law. Eventually an idea grew in Naomi's mind. She realized that Boaz was a distant relative of her and her deceased sons and, as such, had a right under the law to marry Ruth in her widowhood. The custom in Israel at that time (remember, this was a custom that Naomi was comfortable with but one that must have sounded outlandish to Ruth) was that a woman could offer herself in marriage to a man by sleeping at his feet. In this case, the marriage proposal included a requirement that Boaz purchase land that Naomi had inherited from her deceased husband, Elimelech.

So, after both the barley and wheat harvests, Naomi sent Ruth to the place where the men were threshing the grain and where they then slept at night to protect the harvested grain from thieves. She told her to wait until Boaz was asleep, then to uncover his feet and lie down next to them. Naomi didn't even tell Ruth what would happen next; she just told her that Boaz would tell her what to do next.

Talk about trust! Would you trust your mother-in-law enough to do whatever she said just because it was a custom where she came from? Ruth was willing to take the risk and did exactly as Naomi instructed. Sometimes God asks us to take risks. If Ruth could place that much trust in her mother-in-law, shouldn't we be willing to risk obedience to God who loves us, who knows the end from the beginning, and who has our best interest and His glory at heart? Total commitment often involves risk.

Boaz properly interpreted Ruth's actions and offered to become her kinsman-redeemer by buying back the land that had belonged to father-in-law and then marrying her. That way, the family's land would remain in the line that had been broken by the untimely deaths of Elimelech and his sons. Boaz knew the red tape he would have to go through, but he did it, he married Ruth, they took Naomi into their home, they had a baby boy, and they lived happily ever after. But God had a surprise for them.

TUESDAY

Meditation

"The fundamental fact of existence is that this trust in God, this faith, is the firm foundation under everything that makes life worth living. It's our handle on what we can't see."
(Hebrews 11:1 *The Message*)

Meditate on this verse. Think especially about faith, about trust in God. Ask God to show you more about what it really means to have faith in him.

Journal

WEDNESDAY

Thoughts for today:

There's more to Ruth's story, as we see in Matthew 1:5, where Matthew gives for us an accounting of the ancestry of Jesus, the Messiah. God, in his wisdom and perhaps with a touch of divine irony, has included Ruth in the lineage of his own son! She was not even an Israelite. In fact, she was from Moab, a country that was a longstanding enemy of God's own people.

What an honor God gave to Ruth for her commitment to him! Remember that she was a human being just like we are. She was not perfect. I am sure she had bad hair days and bad mood days just as we do. But out of sinful Moab Ruth came to the God of the Bible. God looked at her as an his beloved child and because of her faithfulness to him, included her in the lineage of Jesus Christ. God's choice to honor Ruth wasn't because of who she was; it wasn't because she had special talents (a woman in those days had no education, no legal standing); it certainly wasn't because of her pedigree; it was only because she turned her face toward the God of Israel at a particular point in her life, and she kept her focus on him from that day forward. God richly rewarded Ruth's commitment and consistency.

THURSDAY

Thoughts for today:

Could Ruth have foreseen all of that was to come into her life when she acknowledged the God of Israel as the one true God and chose to follow Naomi to Bethlehem? Of course not! She was not given a revelation of the future, only a sense that the choice she made was the right one and one that she had to follow with all of her heart. She did that, then the next step opened up, then the next, and the next until her life was fully lived out in commitment to the God she came to know and follow. And, as we saw, her obedience did not go unnoticed by God.

As John Eldredge says in *The Journey of Desire*, "Life is not a problem to be solved, but an adventure to be lived" (Thomas Nelson, Inc., 2000, p. 210). How freeing! Ruth is an example to us as to how to live life exactly that way! Does that mean she didn't have any problems? No. She knew hunger, poverty, destitution, discouragement, fatigue, loneliness, and heartache; but she kept following her God one step at a time even when that step required risk. She knew that God was in charge of the outcome which was for her good and his glory. No matter what the circumstances Ruth, at her very core, was devoted to God and to his plan for her life. That's where we want to be, too.

FRIDAY

Reading God's message

Ruth 3

What does this chapter tell us about Ruth's courage to do the right thing? What does it tell us about Boaz? Sometimes God asks us to take a risk, but, if we are following his leading, the risk we take will result in great reward just as it did for Ruth and Boaz.

Journal

SATURDAY

For   personal   reflection

What risk is God asking you to take?

- Does he want you to leave a secure job?
- To enter a new area of service for him?
- To have someone in for dinner?
- To make a difficult phone call?
- To write a long-overdue letter?
- To ask forgiveness from someone whom you have hurt?
- To reach out to the neighbor with cancer?
- To sign up for that art class?

_____

_____

Go ahead, take the risk. If God is leading, it is really not risk at all! He knows the steps that you must take to reap the rewards of a life well lived —a life of purpose, fulfillment, and joy. You won't get there by sitting still. Enjoy your adventure with him!

SUNDAY

Prayer

Your love and light, Lord, have shown me clearly the enemy of my soul; fight for me, Jesus, and hold my hand as we walk the path of righteousness together. You love is better than life.

My prayer:

_____

_____

_____

_____

_____

Taking the Risk

P r i n c i p l e   # 15

God's healing touch can reach only to the buried pains that we are willing to expose. The rest remain buried and unhealed.

Are we ready to entrust our lives to the only one who can bring us meaning and purpose? To turn from lives of self-focus to lives of simple commitment to God? Let's look at some steps we can take in his direction.

At some point Ruth had to consider whether she would remain committed to the gods of Moab or abandon the culture and religion of her own family and choose instead the God of her mother-in-law. I can only imagine that this decision came after an honest evaluation of her life and her heart and a desire to leave the meaningless life of Moab to find fulfillment in Judah, the land of the God of truth. If we want to put our past behind us and allow God to transform us, we have to figure out where we are now. We should not hurry this step in the process. It may take some time to fully evaluate our present condition and to allow the light of the Holy Spirit and the Word of God to reveal the layers of guilt and pain and bitterness that we may have built up over the years.

There was once a Bedouin in the desert who went to the market and purchased a bag of dates. He came back to his tent and, later in the evening, lit a candle, settled in and decided to eat his dates. He reached into the bag, selected a date, and took a bite. It was then that he saw the worm in it and threw it out of the tent. He took a second date and discovered a second worm. He had a problem. He also had a solution. He blew out the candle.

Not a good idea! There are some things about which we dare not remain in the dark. We must be willing to expose our lives to God's light and allow the Holy Spirit to reveal truth and to guide us into a process of healing and growth. Some of us have done exactly what the Bedouin did. We have hurt, pain, or sin in our past and we would rather not deal with it, so it lies buried. Now is the time to dig it up, let God shine the light of his Spirit on it and experience healing. Only when we get rid of the buried past, which is a barrier between us and God, will we be able to see him and hear him clearly.

TUESDAY

Meditation

"Then you will experience for yourselves the truth, and the truth will free you."
(John 8:32 *The Message*)

What does truth mean to you? To God? What does freedom mean to you? To God? Meditate on this verse and ask God to reveal its relevance to your life today.

Journal

WEDNESDAY

Thoughts for today:

In order to learn to cling to our heavenly Father as our sole source of nourishment, strength, and growth, we need to honestly and humbly assess our present spiritual, emotional, and relational conditions. Let me suggest that we find a time to be alone and uninterrupted. We begin self-evaluation in an attitude of prayer before the Father who loves us more than we can comprehend. Then we must commit to being ruthlessly honest with ourselves and with him.

First, we need to get cleaned up. We must ask the Holy Spirit to shine his light in our lives to reveal sins that need to be confessed and forsaken. His revelation will be kind and loving. If he says a habit or a relationship or an action in our lives is sinful, we must agree with him without arguing and rationalizing. Instead, we must confess that sin immediately. There is no sin so attractive that it is worth giving up a fulfilling relationship with God.

We must ask that God himself will overcome that sin in our lives. Willpower won't do it, but willingness to submit to a loving God will. We don't have to try so hard anymore as we learn to yield to God. Once we are clean, we will be ready to move forward into a richer, deeper, more satisfying relationship with God and with others around us.

THURSDAY

Thoughts for today:

After we confess our sins and put our trust in God to strengthen us to stay pure, we need to accept healing for hurts in our past which are still causing pain. We need to ask the Holy Spirit to reveal these hurts to us. As he tenderly shows them to us one by one, we ask him to heal and replenish our wounded souls.

Sometimes God uses other human beings to help us in this healing process. So, if God reveals that our pain will be unearthed and healed only through the help of a Christian counselor, we should call our pastor or a trusted friend for recommended names of counselors. Then we need to make the appointment. If our Father reveals something he wants us to do, we should do it right away so that we can get on with the next assignment he may have for us.

After we get cleaned up and experience healing, we will feel a new intimacy with God. It is logical, then, that the final step in this process is to say thank you. We claim our adoption as God's child and acknowledge that we do have value—not because of our worthiness, holiness, or dedication—only because of the immense worth he has given his children. As we thank him for who he has made us to be, he shares in our joy!

FRIDAY

Reading God's message

Ruth 4

How did God reward Ruth's willingness to take the first step toward him and then to take risks of obedience when he asked her to do so? How did the men and women of Bethlehem respond to Ruth's good fortune? What significance did Ruth and Boaz's child have in the history of our world? Does it give you a sense that God is in control? Doesn't it make you know that you can trust him?

Journal

SATURDAY

For personal reflection

Go through the three steps listed in this section:

1. Get cleaned up: Confess any known sins.
2. Accept healing: Let God show you pain in your life that needs his healing touch.
3. Say thank you: Accept what he does for you and be joyfully grateful for the relationship you now can experience with God and with others.

As you do this, stop to listen to God's voice as he responds to your confession, your prayer for healing, and your offering of thanksgiving. Write down anything you feel he may be directing you to do or any message of encouragement or comfort he may give.

_____

_____

_____

SUNDAY

Prayer

Help me not to be afraid of feeling the pain of my wrong choices, Lord; you will heal them as I choose to put them in the light. Give me the assurance that the pain is only temporary, and the joy is permanent. In your holy name I pray.

My prayer:

_____

_____

_____

_____

_____

Taking Stock

Our personal wholeness and our devotion to God are intricately and irreversibly intertwined.

Ruth's commitment to follow God was so complete that she packed up the little that she owned, left her own family, and followed Naomi to the land of Israel. When Naomi told her to approach Boaz about marriage, she did it courageously, knowing that Naomi was speaking God's will for their lives. If we want God to transform us into the productive, fulfilled men and women he has in mind for us to be, we can do no less. But how does this change occur?

Remember the story of Beauty and the Beast? The prince did not know how to love and, as a result, was cursed; and his entire castle and staff were cursed along with him. He was given a certain amount of time in which to learn how to love. When he fell in love with Belle, his heart was changed, the curse was taken away, and he was transformed back into a handsome young prince. The Beast provides the clue to our transformation: When his heart was right, change followed naturally.

In order for God to change us, our hearts must be right. Trusting him with our lives allows that heart change to occur. I am not talking here about our initial commitment to God in salvation. The type of commitment we are now addressing happens when we realize that we are nothing and he is everything, that we want to get out of the way and let him have more and more control, that we want his will more than we want our own, that we trust him enough to let him lead, knowing that his love for us will be the governing factor in the paths he chooses.

We need to tell him that we want to commit to him on that level. We need to be honest, letting him know if we are not sure how to do it or if we are afraid to take this step. He understands if we tell him that we trust him mostly, but there's a little part of us that needs reassurance.

Our personal wholeness is directly connected to our relationship with God. This initial commitment is a decision that is significant in that we make a conscious choice to turn from following our own ways and, instead, turn our faces toward God as our new leader. Then, over a period of time, our hearts will change and we will become more and more devoted to the God we trust.

TUESDAY

Meditation

"I am...reaching out for Christ, who has so wondrously reached out for me...I've got my eye on the goal, where God is beckoning us onward—to Jesus. I'm off and running, and I'm not turning back. So let's keep focused on that goal, those of us who want everything God has for us."
(Philippians 3:12–15 *The Message*)

Read this passage slowly and thoughtfully. Then meditate on its meaning in your life. Choose a phrase to meditate on throughout today.

Journal

WEDNESDAY

Thoughts for today:

Wholehearted commitment to God sometimes happens when we begin to follow God, but more often the decision for that level of devotion is made at a time when spiritual growth has occurred and our understanding of God and his reign over our lives has reached a more mature level.

Even when we have made an all-out commitment to God, we will find that self takes over little by little and we have to keep pushing self back and giving our lives again to God. And we will find that Satan, as pushy an old demon as he is, will try to take control of areas of our lives; and we will have to shove him away and recommit to God. As we make progress in our Christian lives, we will find that we choose to tell him again and again how much he means to us and how we will make it the goal of our lives to follow him at every step.

Once we have made a heart commitment to God, he has the right, the power, and the authority to transform us into the complete, fulfilled, effective, and astounding people that he has had in mind for us to be all along. The end result is so good, that we would be foolish not to turn to him and let him get started right away!

THURSDAY

Thoughts for today:

Once we have made a decision to become a totally committed follower of God, we must respond when he speaks. We all have friends who are quickly responsive to us and those who are not. Whenever I call or e-mail one particular friend, she may take a day or two to respond as she seems to have to wait until she is "in the mood." Another friend is automatically "in the mood" just because she heard from me. Her answer comes immediately. That's the kind of responsiveness I believe God is looking for in us.

In order for us to respond, we have to know what God expects of us. His moral will is completely revealed in his word. If we read it, study it, memorize it, meditate on it, and live it out in our lives, we will be following God's leading. If we want to know God and know what he expects of us, we have to read and know the book he gave us.

The Bible is full of commands: Each command is a revelation of God's will for us. Are we obeying each of them? The Bible is full of promises: Each promise is a revelation of God's will for us. Are we claiming each of them in faith? We have a lot to do and a lot to gain as we stay connected to him!

FRIDAY

Reading God's message

Ephesians 4

What instructions for Christian living does Paul give in this passage? What characteristics does he say we should exhibit as Christ followers? What goals does he describe in Verse 13? What is the new self like that we are told to put on in Verse 24. How should we treat other believers? In Verses 15–16, Paul tells us what the source of this new life is—it is our connection to Christ. This is not a self-improvement program. It is a description of what our lives will be like as we stay connected to Christ, our spiritual head. It is a description of God's will for us.

Journal

SATURDAY

For personal reflection

Write out a prayer of commitment, surrender, and submission to God and pray it every day for the next month.

_____

_____

_____

_____

Renew your commitment to God frequently. Sometimes the prayer must be prayed moment by moment as you go through your day. Over time, the commitment becomes more ingrained and repetition will not be as frequent.

But for now, write it down and pray it often!

SUNDAY

Prayer

Father, forgive the times when I ignore you or leave you out. I know this hurts you and it also hurts me. Thank you for your quick forgiveness—no pouting or temper tantrums from you. Continue to renew my mind. I ask this in Jesus' holy name. Amen.

My prayer:

_____

_____

_____

_____

Giving All to God

P r i n c i p l e   # 17

The life of the Spirit does not mean perfection, but it means continually moving toward that goal.

As God changes us, we want more and more to do his will. One way in which God's will for us is revealed is through the Bible. But he shows us what he wants in other ways, as well. When people say they do not know what God wants them to do, I will often respond with this question: Have you asked him? Isaiah 8:19 says, "Should not a people inquire of their God?" God is in the business of revealing his will. He wants us to know what it is, but we have to search Scriptures and we have to ask him to direct us.

Have you heard the story of Mary Ghee? Mary was a missionary in India who learned how to listen to God. She would enter into prayer with her heavenly Father and then, with notebook and pencil in hand, would present an issue or a problem to him and ask for direction. Because she was in an attitude of prayer and had quieted her own voices within her head, she would accept by faith that any direction coming to her was coming from God. She would write down the thoughts that came, then she would obey the direction given. Exciting changes came about in the effectiveness of her ministry in India. She was a quiet, unassuming woman, but people began to come from miles around to pray with her and to obtain from God the direction he gave through her. *We* have the same access to God that Mary had.

If we are seeking God sincerely in prayer, spending time in his presence, and waiting for him to speak (We too often do all the talking!), he will reveal to us what he wants us to do. We will be surprised at how it becomes easier and easier to hear him as we practice living in his presence, seeking out quiet moments with him, and keeping the channels clear and uncluttered so we can hear him speak.

When God reveals something for us do to either in his word or by revelation during our time of prayer, we must do it as soon as possible. He will not reveal the next step or the next or the next until we follow the direction he has already given. We will be blocked from further spiritual growth and transformation until we respond to what he tells us to do.

TUESDAY

Meditation

"All the things I once thought were so important are gone from my life. Compared to the high privilege of knowing Christ Jesus as my Master, first-hand, everything I once thought I had going for me is insignificant—dog dung. I've dumped it all in the trash so that I could embrace Christ and be embraced by him."
(Philippians 3:8 *The Message*)

Let God speak to you through this testimony of the Apostle Paul. Are you getting to a point in your spiritual walk where some of this is your testimony, too? Meditate on the message that God has for you in this verse.

Journal

WEDNESDAY

Thoughts for today:

We simply need to accept the direction God has given even if it doesn't make total sense to us. God's pattern is to reveal his plan and his will one step at a time. Why? Because he wants us to live by faith, to live in complete reliance on him. We don't have to have much faith if we have the entire road map. We do need to exercise faith, however, if we know only the next step we have to take.

What is God asking you to do? By this point in our study together, you probably know the answer to that question. It may seem like a very small thing—but you will never know how that small thing will meet a need in someone else's life, will set a direction for you or someone you love, or will open up communication between you and God—unless you take that first step.

As we obey day by day and keep our focus on God, we can trust that he will bring about the transformation in us that he desires. We have to keep remembering that it's not about us. If God wants us to be changed, he will change us. We don't have to do it ourselves. Our job is to stay committed to him. *That we can* do.

THURSDAY

Thoughts for today:

An effective spiritual journey is made up of one small act of obedience after another. Let's look at the steps in the journey of commitment that Jesus gives in Luke 9:23:

- *Deny yourself.* That means that we are not the ones we should be thinking about. We already have learned that our focus should be directed outward and upward, not inward.
- *Take up your cross daily.* Each day we begin again with the responsibilities and burdens of our lives. Life is made up of days and hours. Transformation does not happen without going through the daily grind.
- *Follow Me.* If we keep our eyes on Christ and follow where he leads, we cannot go in a wrong direction!

What do we sometimes do instead of taking these three steps?

- We indulge ourselves. We think that just this once won't matter.
- We try daily to escape the burdens and responsibilities of our lives or we complain about having to deal with them.
- We keep our focus on ourselves rather than on Jesus, our leader.

No wonder we feel like spiritual failures! We are not doing it his way! Today is the day to change that. We must do what God says, believe that his plan will be brought about in our lives, and turn toward him in total commitment.

FRIDAY

Reading God's message

Matthew 6:25–34

These verses tell us more about living our life God's way. What commands does Jesus give in this passage? What examples does he give of God's special care for us? What promises does he give? What priorities does he set for us in Verse 33?

Journal

SATURDAY

For personal reflection

Let's stop to evaluate how you are doing in the spiritual walk that we have been engaged in through these lessons:

From what sins have you been forgiven?

What new truths have you been able to apply to your life?

What have you learned about yourself?

What steps of obedience have you taken?

Have you been able to sense and follow God's direction and experience his loving presence?

Thank God for the direction in which you are moving and recommit yourself to continuing to cling to him so that he can change you into all that he has in mind for you to be.

SUNDAY

Prayer

Father, I put my old ways of thinking, feeling, and doing into your hands and will wait to receive back your life in the Spirit. I will practice patience with myself and have mercy on me as you have mercy on me. With your help, I will be free to be me.

My prayer:

_____

_____

_____

_____

_____

Learning to Respond

P r i n c i p l e   # 18

**In order to come to the end of our lives in satisfied fulfillment, we must
stay in touch with God's Spirit within us today.**

We all know that our days are numbered. We have a limited period of time on
earth in order to become what God wants us to be. We have only so many
years to accomplish our goals and to relate effectively to those who are dear
to us. We acknowledge that life is made up of one day at at a time. It is what
we do with the minutes and hours that eventually add up to the full measure
of our lives. We all know people who have grown older and bemoan lost
years, years that were wasted on efforts that have no long-lasting value, years
that were spent in leaving broken relationships unaddressed, and years that
were lived without knowledge of God. What a tragedy. It is a sad story, but
one that can be avoided.

If you and I have been walking in commitment to God, we are beyond wasted
lives. We have found meaning in relationship with our heavenly Father and
we have begun to experience his healing touch in our lives. The way we spend
our time is now different. The relationships we have are beginning to change.
Our hearts are softened toward spiritual matters. Our eyes are opened to
matters that are important for eternity. Let's think now of what the end of our
lives will bring. Think of the joys of looking back at a life well lived, one that
has been productive for God's kingdom, and one that has brought us fulfillment and earned God's approving smile.

Ruth has been a good example to us. When, as an old woman, she reviewed
her life, I imagine she saw that once she chose to follow God he met every
need of her life physically, emotionally, and spiritually. She simply needed to
choose to be obedient to him and to trust him to bring about the transformation that he desired for her. Her trust was rewarded lavishly.

We all want to get to the end of our lives and remember when we simply,
but sincerely, made a full commitment to the God who loves us more than we
can know. No matter what our age, there is still time to live for God, still time
to make the end of our lives satisfying and fulfilling, still time to prepare for
an eternity living in the love of the triune God and all of his children. Using
Ruth as an example, let's take a look together at what we need to do in order
to finish the race of life with joy, satisfaction, and triumph.

TUESDAY

Meditation

"God's Way is not a matter of mere talk; it's an empowered life."
(I Corinthians 4:20 *The Message*)

Meditate on the concept of an empowered life. What message does God have for you in this verse today?

Journal

WEDNESDAY

Thoughts for today:

What do you suppose Ruth saw when she, as an old woman, reflected on the life she had lived?

She remembered meeting the unusual family from Bethlehem, marrying one of their sons, and learning of their God. She remembered how she followed the God of her mother-in-law out of Moab and into Judah. She remembered how God had taken her heart of grief after the loss of her husband and filled it with a new love for and from Boaz. She remembered how God graciously took her from destitution and poverty into a position of comfort and security. She remembered the joy of the birth of Obed and later of her grandson, Jesse.

What she did not know by the time she died was that her great grandson, David, would rule Israel as king and that God would raise up from David's line the long-promised Messiah who would bring redemption to the world.

Eventually the day came when Ruth died. She was mourned here on earth, but because she had followed God so closely, the step of death was a small one for her. It was just one more way of submitting to the God she had learned to trust. Then, I imagine God joyfully showing Ruth the great role that her son and future offspring would play in bringing the world an opportunity for right relationship with him. God is a God of happy surprises!

T H U R S D A Y

T h o u g h t s   f o r   t o d a y :

Unless God takes us to heaven sooner, we will all find ourselves someday in that proverbial rocking chair looking back on a life made up of hours and days. Put yourself now in that chair and visualize what you might see when you get to the end of your life. What will it be? One failure after another? Years of frustration and anxiety? Dissatisfaction and unfulfilled longings? Loneliness and broken relationships? Insecurity and self doubt?

It doesn't have to be that way. There's still time to move in God's direction and change what you will see when you are an old man or an old woman. If you are willing to walk close to God, you will look back and remember the step of obedience you took when you had no idea *why* he was asking you to do what he directed, and you will see:

- how that first step led to another,
- how your heart became softer,
- how a relationship began to change,
- how you grew in your love for others and in your ability to reach out to help them, and
- how you fell in love more and more with the God in whom you had placed your trust.

You will smile and pray and wonder how you ever thought you could live your life any other way.

F R I D A Y

R e a d i n g   G o d ' s   m e s s a g e

II Timothy 3:10–4:8

These are Paul's last words. He was about to die (V. 4:6) and he knew it. Now he wants to pass the leadership of God's work on to Timothy, a young man whom he had mentored for many years. Read Paul's instructions to Timothy. What do these instructions tell us about what is important to Paul in his final hours? See how Paul views his life with satisfaction. Note the reward that he expects from his Lord. Paul died well because he lived well. Let us pray to be able to do the same.

J o u r n a l

SATURDAY

F o r   p e r s o n a l   r e f l e c t i o n

Have you ever thought about what you would like written on your grave-stone? For what do you want your family and friends to remember you?

Reduce that memory to a few words and make it the goal of each day to live in such a way that when you are gone, you will be remembered as you had desired.

If you're not sure of what that remembrance goal should be, ask God to show you what his desire is for the purpose and meaning of your life. Then write it down, put it into practice, and allow him to bring it about as you live your life moment by moment.

SUNDAY

P r a y e r

Holy Spirit, tell me what I ought to do and command me to do it. I promise to submit to whatever you permit to happen to me today, only show me what is your will.

My prayer:

The Radical Results

P r i n c i p l e   # 19

Our faith is effective only if the one in whom we have placed it is both powerful and loving.

What do you do when there is no one to trust anymore? You are drowning and going down for the third time. You are gulping water. Breathing has become a foreign concept. You just let go and feel yourself sinking to the bottom of the lake. No, wait! You are not sinking. You begin to feel buoyant in the water. Someone is under you, pushing you upwards. You break through the surface of the water and drink in the fresh air above the waves. You have survived. You have been saved even though you had let go, you had given up hope.

Trust comes in when you finally figure out that it is not all up to you anymore. In fact, the less it can be up to you and the more helpless you feel, the more likely rock-bottom trust will show up. Trust is funny that way—if you don't need it, it's hard to find. How does this concept apply to your spiritual life? If you can grow spiritually on your own, if you can pretty well understand the Bible, if you have a fairly good grasp of the character of God, then you really don't need a lot of trust. But if you stumble now and then in your spiritual walk, if the Bible is sometimes confusing, if life's problems pile up until you feel you can't breathe, and if God's direction in your life is more mysterious than it is clear, then you need trust—lots of it. The good news is that God is in the business of giving it—just as much as we need.

Have you ever been in a situation when you felt that everything familiar had been taken away? You lost a job? You lost a child? You lost a spouse? You lost a parent? You lost face? You lost prestige? Those kinds of losses in our lives serve a purpose. They uncover the truth that we have been trusting in something that can be shaken, can be removed, can be lost. What then? How do you figure out whom or what you can trust? Even more fundamental, what is the kind of trust we are so in need of?

Essentially, we must give up relying totally on ourselves or on people and things of this world to keep us and to satisfy us and, instead, we must discover the life of trusting God who is totally and unfailingly trustworthy.

TUESDAY

Meditation

"The One who called you is completely dependable. If he said it, he'll do it!"
(I Thessalonians 5:24 *The Message*)

Is there a promise that God has given you? Claim it as yours. Trust him to bring it about. Think about God's trustworthiness; then meditate on the words of this Scripture. Allow the Holy Spirit to comfort your heart and to increase your faith in God with these words.

Journal

WEDNESDAY

Thoughts for today:

Faith that God honors requires that we not rely on our own efforts. We have been taught from earliest childhood to do it ourselves—learn, do, grow, become independent. So, now we pride ourselves on our self sufficiency; we are good decision makers, we can figure things out on our own. We have learned to place our trust in ourselves, in our efforts, in our abilities, and in others around us.

Then something happens that is bigger than we are and we find that the reliability of the object of our faith is what really matters. If you trusted your husband and he abandons you and the children, does that mean your faith was not strong enough? No, it means that your faith had the wrong target.

If your child is diagnosed with a life-threatening disease and you are in a panic, does that mean that your faith has failed? No, it means that your trust was focused on earthly values and maybe even on medical science.

If you had trust that your employer would keep you financially secure, and the company folds, does that mean your faith was too weak? No, it means that your trust was directed toward the writer of the check, not toward the true supplier of your needs.

As someone once said, "We don't know that Jesus is all that we need until Jesus is all that we've got." Have you placed your trust in someone who cannot and will not let you down?

THURSDAY

Thoughts for today:

Who or what is a safe object of your ultimate trust? Probably not a human being. Although we learn to trust each other, it is always with the knowledge that people change, circumstances change, and there are times when we let each other down. We know that our trust should not be in money. Financial resources are transient and, although it is tempting to trust in them, it doesn't take long to figure out that money will not provide the real security that we need. Maybe the only one that you can trust is yourself. After all, you won't let you down. Or will you? In reality, we fail to live up to our own expectations of ourselves all the time.

As we learn to discern the character of God, we find that he is all-loving. He will never do anything that will not be for our best good. Not only that, he is all-powerful. In other words, he has the ability to guide us, protect us, enable us, and provide for us.

If God were all loving but not powerful, he may not be able to keep his promises even though his loving heart would want to. If God were all powerful, but not loving, we would (appropriately) live in horrified fear of him.

But because he loves us unconditionally and because he has the power to do what he determines is good for us, God alone is completely trustworthy.

FRIDAY

Reading God's message

Psalm 86

How does David describe himself in this prayer? What does he ask God to do? How does he describe God? What does David promise to do to honor God? What kind of attitude does David have toward God? Is there anything in this psalm that speaks to your present situation? Is there an attitude that you may need to change? Is there a prayer that you need to pray?

Journal

SATURDAY

For personal reflection

Did you ever consider yourself as an untrustworthy person? Maybe you don't intend to be, but if you compare yourself to God, you have to admit you fall far short in terms of reliability.

Think about your life and make a list of areas (*e.g.* job, children, marriage, finances, addictions) in which you are relying on yourself when you should be relying on God instead.

Since you know that God is more trustworthy than you are, turn those areas over to him and trust that he will handle them to your benefit and his glory!

Keep repeating this commitment over the next few weeks or months to insure that you don't take back what you have given to God. It takes reinforcement to break the habit of handling things ourselves. Give these life issues to him again and again and again until you really trust that he has a firm grip on them and you can let them go!

SUNDAY

Prayer

Lord, you are my only reality; you have shown yourself to be trustworthy and have given me your authenticity. Help me to be a good soldier as I bear your name to those around me in the battleground of everyday life. I ask in your name, Jesus.

My prayer:

_____

_____

_____

_____

_____

It's Who You Trust That Counts

P r i n c i p l e   # 20

Having a problem you cannot solve will either turn you bitter or turn you to God.

Sometimes it is when our self-provided securities are removed that we discover the need to redirect our trust to someone who will never let us down. When crisis comes into our lives, and it will, the crisis becomes a test of where or in whom we have placed our trust.

Have you ever faced a problem you could not figure out how to solve? For example, what would you do if you were told that you have cancer? All of a sudden, things are out of your control. Maybe you have dealt with that issue with yourself or with someone you love. You can panic, or despair, or rail at God for not taking care of you. Or you can learn to trust him on a deeper, more dependent level while relying on his step-by-step direction.

Here is an example of a conscious decision that our family made to place our trust in someone who we believed to be a trustworthy guide through a crisis in our lives. Our daughter Tarah, a bright college senior about to embark on her independent adult life, was diagnosed with cancer. What did we do?

First, we needed someone who knew more about fighting this disease than we did. We needed someone we could trust to make the best possible medical decisions for her. So we met with the best oncologist we could find and decided that we would do everything he said. We consciously and simply put our trust in his wisdom and training while knowing that it is God who is the ulimate healer.

A few weeks earlier, did we ever imagine we would be making an appointment with an oncologist? No. Did we need to trust him at that time? No. But when we needed someone in whom to place confidence, this physician was recommended and we made a choice to trust him. Little did we know how that trust was to be tested over the next few months.

Sometimes God puts us into a position when we are helpless and it seems that trust is our only choice. That's when we learn that we can take him at his word, and we find that in all cases he proves himself to be trustworthy even when the rest of our world seems to be turning upside down. We would like to be able to say, as Job did, "Though he slay me, yet I hope in him." (Job 13:15a). He knew the object of his faith and that object was reliable, worthy of trust, and unshakeable.

TUESDAY

Meditation

"I've learned by now to be quite content whatever my circumstances. I'm just as happy with little as with much, with much as with little. I've found the recipe for being happy whether full or hungry, hands full or hands empty. Whatever I have, wherever I am, I can make it through anything in the One who makes me who I am."

(Philippians 4:11–13 *The Message*)

Meditate on this verse. Think about all that Paul had to go through in his life in order to get to the point where he could honestly make these statements. Think about the role that trust in a loving God plays in being able to agree with Paul concerning contentment and happiness.

Journal

WEDNESDAY

Thoughts for today:

Tarah's doctor seemed competent and had all the accoutrements that went with success, so it was pretty easy to trust him when we were sitting in his professionally outfitted office discussing the treatment plan he outlined.

But there were trials ahead that tested our faith in him. First came the lumpectomy to remove the tumor. The result? Pain! Bleeding, swelling, drains, medications. But we still trusted that the doctor knew what he was doing, and we moved ahead with the next course of treatment: chemotherapy.

The treatments caused weakness, nausea, hair loss, and overall malaise. There were times when our daughter's trust in the oncologist faltered and she had to be reassured that the chemo was for her good in spite of contrary evidence.

Have you ever sat in church on Sunday morning and felt that your faith was strong, your relationship with God was good, and there was nothing that you and he could not tackle together? Then comes the rest of the week, each day bringing its own problems. What happens to your faith then? Do you begin to doubt God? Do you begin to wonder if he is good after all?

Just as we had to continue to trust the doctor although the treatments he sent Tarah's way were difficult and full of pain, you and I have to continue to trust God even when we cannot see or understand why he would allow us to experience the suffering we face.

T H U R S D A Y

T h o u g h t s   f o r   t o d a y :

For Tarah, radiation followed the chemotherapy. It would have been a lot easier to give up at this point instead of going through radiation that made her tired, made her skin burn, and took too much time for a busy college senior. But we kept reminding ourselves that the oncologist knew what he was doing and with faith in him and God, she saw the treatments through to the end.

None of what Tarah went through seemed good at the time she was experiencing it. The disease did not make her feel bad—only the treatments did. But they were treatments, trials, and troubles that were accepted as necessary and life-giving because we knew that the physician who sent them our way had her best interests at heart.

When she received the news at the end of the treatment, "You are now cancer free," we felt that the difficulties were worth the struggle; and the pain and discomfort for her are becoming less vivid memories as time goes on.

The day will come when our trials will be over. If we choose to trust God instead of becoming angry and bitter, he will see us through the difficulties and make us stronger, purer, more satisfied, and more useful to his kingdom. Someday God will welcome us into his heaven where we will live with him forever and the pains we experience now will fade far into the distance.

F R I D A Y

R e a d i n g   G o d ' s   m e s s a g e

Hebrews 11

This chapter of the Bible has been called "Faith's Hall of Fame." The people honored in this chapter are revered for the life of faith that they lived in spite of not receiving in this world the rewards for their faithfulness. Make a list of the names of those who are honored in this chapter. Think about what you know about their lives. What kinds of things did they have to accept in faith? What kinds of difficulties did they suffer (see Verses 35–39) in this world? Imagine what kind of trusting relationship they had with God in order to keep on being obedient even when they could not see the positive results of what they were doing.

J o u r n a l

SATURDAY

For personal reflection

In what do you find it easy to place your trust?
- Your job for the paycheck it brings?
- Your spouse for the emotional support he/she provides?
- Our country for the safety and security that our protected borders give?
- Or yourself because no one cares quite as much as you do about your own well-being?

Here's news: God cares about you *more* than you do and he combines his power with his love for you to bring about the best in your life. Trust God with everything that comes along.

Pray a prayer of commitment to him now. Then, learn to breathe prayers all day long committing your time, your circumstances, and your relationships to him. Commit to allowing suffering in your life without demanding that God will take it away. Instead trust that he is working a work of grace and healing through the pain you experience. Then step back and trust him with the outcome.

SUNDAY

Prayer

O divine Master, you have taught me to not be anxious about anything but in everything with prayer let my requests be made known to you. Your promise of peace follows and that is where I want to dwell. I am your obedient learner.

My prayer:

_____

_____

_____

_____

_____

Faith's Focus

P r i n c i p l e   # 21

Getting to know God is getting to know that he is trustworthy.

I think we can agree that the first step in this life of faith is to establish a relationship with God before we face a faith-testing crisis. Job did this. He is described in the opening verses of the biblical book that bears his name as "a righteous man." He worshiped God and made sacrifices for himself and his children. He had developed a relationship of trust in God far in advance of the troubles that came into his life. Just as we would investigate the reputation of a doctor or a lawyer before we willingly put our faith in their advice, Job had developed a relationship history with God that assured him that God was, in fact, worthy of unwavering trust, even when Job was in the middle of a nightmare not knowing when—or if—he would ever wake up.

You probably know the story. God and Job are doing pretty well together, but Satan challenged God by stating that Job trusted God only because he had blessed him with so many wonderful things. God knew better. He knew Job and knew that Job would pass any test that Satan put in his path. So God gave Satan permission to tamper with some of the things and people in which Satan thought Job had placed his trust.

Without his knowing why, Job's enviable circumstances suddenly reversed. One-by-one, the things and people that Job had counted on in his life were taken away: his children, his possessions, his servants, his financial security, and even his health. But in losing all of the stuff of life, Job found that his real trust was not in those things or in those people, though he loved them dearly. His undying trust had been and remained in God alone and never wavered during the times of great stress and loss in his life. That trust saw him through the suffering, the pain, the heartache, and the grief. He felt it all. He mourned the loss of his children. He grieved when his servants were killed. He was vulnerable when his financial resources were taken away.

He continued to trust in God's wisdom and goodness even when evidence seemed to point to a God who was unreliable and unloving. He was able to maintain this faith because, long before these terrible difficulties came along, Job had established a relationship with God and knew he could rely on God's unchanging character.

TUESDAY

Meditation

"It's impossible to please God apart from faith. And why? Because anyone who wants to approach God must believe both that he exists and that he cares enough to respond to those who seek him."
(Hebrews 11:6 *The Message*)

What does this verse tell you to believe about God? Think about how this pleases him. Meditate on the teaching on faith that this passage provides.

Journal

WEDNESDAY

Thoughts for today:

If we would like to be as prepared as Job was to handle the crises that will come into our lives, we need to get to know God as well as Job knew him. What do we know about the character of God? Here are some ways to find out more:

1. *God is revealed through Jesus.* We are told this about Jesus in Hebrews 1:3: "The Son is the radiance of God's glory and the exact representation of his being." In other words, if we know what Jesus is like, we will know what God is like. When we read about the life of Christ in the Bible, we find out about his personality, about his dealings with people, and about his relationship with God in heaven.

2. *God is revealed in his creation.* If we spend time in God's creation, we learn about him. We marvel at his love of color, shapes, patterns, sizes, diversity, and detail.

3. *God is revealed to us through prayer.* We need to talk to him freely about our lives and our concerns. We need to offer him praise and adoration and listen for the internal response of the Holy Spirit. The more we get to know him, the more we realize how good he is, how loving, and how perfectly trustworthy.

T H U R S D A Y

T h o u g h t s   f o r   t o d a y :

In order for us to have a fuller knowledge of God, we first must believe that he is a good and loving God and that he will reward our seeking him. God is not hiding. He wants us to find him, to trust him, to know him. What do we already know about God? He is all loving, all merciful, full of kindness, gentleness, and grace. He does not get impatient with us. Even when he corrects us, the correction is done out of a depth of love that we cannot fathom, but that we can feel.

Our trust in God opens the floodgates from him to us so that we will experience his love, his tenderness, and his mercy as we have never experienced it before. We first must accept in faith that he is who he has proved himself to be. God never changes. He cannot be malicious, uncaring, or capricious because to act in those ways would go against his very nature.

If we look at God with a lack of understanding about who he really is, we will not be receptive to his loving advances toward us. Instead, because we have been let down in human relationships, we will question him, doubt his motives, and suspect that he really doesn't love us. The better we know him, the more our faith will grow because we will find him to be completely worthy of our trust.

F R I D A Y

R e a d i n g   G o d ' s   m e s s a g e

Psalm 139

Read this psalm and write down all the characteristics of God that it reveals. What kind of reaction to God does the psalmist show? What requests does the writer make of God? What is your favorite part of the psalm? Why?

J o u r n a l

SATURDAY

For personal reflection

Think of ways in which you can get to know God better.

Spending more time in Bible reading and study.
Devoting more time to prayer.
Learning more about meditation.
Studying nature to see how God has revealed himself in creation.
Focusing on the life of Christ to see how Jesus revealed what the Father
is like.

After you think of a way to know God better that captures *your* attention,
begin today to put it into practice. Begin a notebook or journal page in which
you write down everything you learn about God, his character, and his relationship to us as humans.

SUNDAY

Prayer

As you speak to me, Lord Jesus, I can hear your voice of love and tenderness.
Give me your discernment, Holy Spirit, to recognize the other voices in my
head that are not coming from love. I need you, I want you. Accept my love in
Jesus' name. Amen.

My prayer:

_____

_____

_____

_____

_____

*Know Who You
Can Count On*

Principle # 22

We don't have to have all the answers.
We just have to know the one who does.

Have you ever been accused of being a control freak? Many of us have! But, an important step in the faith process is *giving up* control. We have already acknowledged that faith comes when we realize we cannot live life by our own efforts. Remember the drowning person we described? We have all read stories about someone who is drowning, flailing and fighting so strongly that he foils the attempts of others to rescue him. We need to stop fighting and stop protesting the problems we encounter and let ourselves be rescued.

When we know God and his character, we are more likely to allow him to have control of our lives. We simply trust him to be on our side during the difficulties we face. We know from the depths of our being that, although we want to escape the pain we are going through, he knows better than we do what will be for our ultimate good.

Giving up control means giving up the right to know the reasons for the trials in our lives. Sometimes the first question that comes to our minds when we are facing troubles is sort of a whiny protest, "Why me? After all, I'm a good person. What have I done to deserve this?" This is not a totally inappropriate question to ask, but we need to be asking it not in protest, but in true query concerning what we need to correct in our lives or what we need to learn from our difficult experiences.

Job didn't know that he was the target of the greater battle of good and evil, a battle between God and Satan. After some genuine sorrowing about the losses he experienced and after some commiseration with his friends, Job concludes that he will have unwavering trust in God even if God goes so far as to take his life. Because of that unequivocal trust, Job didn't demand an answer as to why all this was happening to him. He was human, though, and he did ask God for enlightenment about what was going on. God gave replies that told Job that he was in control, that he was sovereign, and that the only appropriate response for a human being to have toward God is one of submission and trust. When we submit to God, trusting in his unchanging and ever-loving character, we are free from the burden of being in control.

TUESDAY

Meditation

"Humble yourselves, therefore, under God's mighty hand that he may lift you up in due time."
(I Peter 5:6)

Meditate on the meaning of humility. Allow the Holy Spirit to teach your spirit what humility means from God's point of view. Then focus on the promise given in this verse and ask God to make that promise a part of your very being.

Journal

WEDNESDAY

Thoughts for today:

Think of the freedom we experience when we turn over control of our lives to God. We can
- stop trying so hard.
- stop trying to live up to other people's expectations.
- stop trying to fix all the things that are wrong in our lives.
- stop being stressed out.
- stop feeling so responsible for everything that happens.
- stop being self-critical.
- stop worrying about everything around us that we cannot control or change.

We know that God can do nothing toward us that does not flow out of love. So we trust him. We listen for his voice, we experience his presence, we are honest with him about our feelings, and we look forward to growing in our relationship to him and to others through the difficult times.

We experience true freedom when we begin to set our minds on God and on his sovereign control of our lives and of the world around us. We are free when we set our hearts on doing his will, following his voice, and pleasing him alone. Why would we want to sail the ship of our lives when the one who built the ship and created the seas on which it sails is willing to steer us through the storms that will come? Does it make more sense to count on ourselves or on God?

THURSDAY

Thoughts for today:

When we experience suffering, we are wise if we approach God humbly to ask him if there is a disciplinary reason for the problems we face. We know from Scripture (Hebrews 12:5–7) that sometimes we undergo problems or hardships due to our need for discipline.

If God is bringing trials into our lives as a way of bringing us back to him, we will know what we have done that needs correction and what God is trying to accomplish through the discipline. Just as a loving parent will not punish a child without the child knowing why he is being punished, so God will not bring discipline into our lives without our knowing why.

If we ask God what it is he wants to teach us, he will tell us. He is neither vicious nor capricious and will not bring disciplinary measures to us without our having the opportunity to learn from the experience. If the Holy Spirit brings conviction to our hearts, we simply confess the sin to God in prayer, repent of the wrongdoing, and begin to walk in renewed fellowship with him. On the other hand, if no sin is brought to mind by the Holy Spirit, then we can safely assume that the trials in our lives are there for reasons that we may not know in this lifetime, but we can be confident that they are not sent by God as punishment.

FRIDAY

Reading God's message

Hebrews 12

According to this chapter, who is our example as we run this race of life? What does this passage teach us about God's discipline in our lives? What will be the result in our lives of this kind of training? What regret can sin cause in our lives according to Verses 14–17? What do the last eleven verses tell us about God's power and majesty?

Journal

SATURDAY

For personal reflection

What areas of your life are important for you to control?

What areas do you willingly give up to others?

Consciously and humbly give over to God whatever it is that is hardest to give up: Your children? Your financial security? Your personal safety? Your eternal life? Your job? Approval from others?

Whatever you identify, give it up. Let God have it. Yield it to him today—and, if necessary, again tomorrow and the next day until you no longer want to control. Trust him to do a better job with it than you did! List here what you give up to God:

_____

_____

_____

SUNDAY

Prayer

Heavenly Father, help me to practice being outside of time as you are; give me assurance that the answer will come in your way and at the right time, whenever that may be. While I am waiting on you, we will have fun together.

My prayer:

_____

_____

_____

_____

_____

Knowing What to Ask

P r i n c i p l e   # 23

Our suffering is the stethoscope through which we hear the heartbeat of God.

When we believe that there is purpose in what we are suffering, our troubles are much more bearable. In fact, God, in order to encourage our faith, tells us what that purpose is in Romans 5:3–4 (*The Message*), "…we know how troubles can develop passionate patience in us, and how that patience in turn forges the tempered steel of virtue, keeping us alert for whatever God will do next."

Just think of the day Job died and entered heaven's gates. I'm sure God was more than eager to explain to Job why the horrible atrocities happened in his lifetime. It was a cosmic battle that brought those devastating problems to Job, a battle that Job was not privy to during this earthly existence. When he found out, I'm sure it was an "Aha" moment for him.

Romans 4:16 in *The Message* says, "…the fulfillment of God's promise depends entirely on trusting God and his way, and then simply embracing him and what he does." That's what Job did. He trusted God, allowed God to do what he wished to do in his world, and embraced God—hanging on to him for all he was worth through the roller coaster ride of his life. That's what faith is—figuring out that it is God we can trust and then hanging on to him and letting him hang on to us. God, and God alone, is worthy of that kind of trust. We don't have to make it any more complicated than that.

We also need to keep an eternal perspective. This life, as C. S. Lewis reflected, is only shadows of the real life which is yet to come. But it takes faith to believe in the life beyond this world and in the eternal values that that real life represents. We can't see it now or experience it; we simply have to believe that there is a heaven and that Jesus meant it when he said he was going to prepare a place for us and would come back someday to take us to live with him.

We have to accept in faith that the events of this world and our reaction to them prepare us for the eternal life, which is of infinitely greater significance and infinitely greater duration than the life we are experiencing now. If we believe that, truly believe it, our earthly problems take on a whole new perspective.

TUESDAY

Meditation

"Consider it a sheer gift, friends, when tests and challenges come at you from all sides. You know that under pressure, your faith-life is forced into the open and shows its true colors. So don't try to get out of anything prematurely. Let it do its work so you become mature and well-developed, not deficient in any way."
(James 1:2–4 *The Message*)

Meditate on what this passage tells you about the purpose of suffering in your life.

Journal

WEDNESDAY

Thoughts for today:

Trials encourage us to become totally focused on God and his activity in our lives. We grow through difficulties knowing that God will be revealed to us through our suffering. We find him in the middle of the storm.

There will be evident changes in us if we are living this kind of faith life. Probably the most obvious is that we will walk around with spirits that are calmer and more peaceful than they used to be, thankful to the God of the universe for loving us even when life may be falling apart around us. At first, people may think we just don't understand the magnitude of our problems. If we did understand, we would be fretting and worrying as they do instead of moving through our difficult circumstances with an underlying joy and a thankful heart. When the focus of our lives is God, he receives honor even in the middle of our difficult circumstances.

Our lives become silent arrows directing people's attention to the God we trust. If we persist in trusting God, those around us will move on from expressing sympathy about our circumstances and will, instead, be pointed toward God. Then God will receive glory because of our gratitude and because of the supernatural peace that he gives in exchange for our faith in him. The focus is redirected from us to God, who alone deserves praise!

THURSDAY

Thoughts for today:

There are many benefits that come to us as we live out our lives of faith. One is that we have more emotional energy to give to others. When we trust God with our problems and accept the peace he gives in return, we are more able to come alongside those who need our help and our love.

Also, learning to trust God expands our understanding as to whom we can trust on a human level. As we learn to know God and his character, we look for similar characteristics in people around us. When we recognize those characteristics, we know whom we can trust and to what extent. Our entire trust life is thus protected and directed by God.

We get to choose whom we will trust. We can choose to have faith in the one who is most trustworthy and who, by his very character, will do and allow only what is best for us. We trust him for the outcome even when evidence seems against him. God is the only one who will never let us down, who has our best interests at heart, who sees the end of the story even in the middle of all the chaos, and who has the power to bring about good out of the circumstances in which we find ourselves. We can choose a sure thing!

FRIDAY

Reading God's message

Psalm 37

Make two lists as you read this psalm. List all the commands and all of the promises. What do you learn about God's love? What do you learn about his power? Does this passage help you to trust God more?

Journal

SATURDAY

For personal reflection

In going through this study, what reasons have you found to trust God?

___

How have you learned to know him better?

___

Do you want to be closer to him?

___

What has he done in your life or in the lives of those you know to prove himself trustworthy?

___

Remind yourself of God's great track record when you are tempted not to trust!

SUNDAY

Prayer

You have my attention now, Lord. Give me the next step to take that will lead me closer to you. Help me to put my feet in your footprints. Keep me from the danger that is waiting to envelope me. Send your holy angels to minister to me. I give you thanks and praise for always hearing me, your loving, hurting child.

My prayer:

___

___

___

___

Keep Your Eye on the Outcome

P r i n c i p l e   # 24

Real life begins when we learn to experience the present moment.

It is now 7:30 a.m., we have meetings that are hours away, but we are thinking about them already. We anticipate appointments and duties to be accomplished. Our day is planned, and we awaken with our thoughts and energies already going into those plans. But what about the present moment? Do we lose the joys, the blessings, the experience of 7:30 by thinking forward to noon and 1:30 and 3:00?

Now, we sense the presence of God because we just finished our devotional time reading passages of Scripture, meditating on his greatness, and allowing the overflow of the Holy Spirit to be felt in our innermost beings.

Now, we feel the coolness of the morning and the freshness of the air around us as we sit in the early sunlit hours of a new day.

Now, we experience the renewed energy provided by having had a good night's rest.

Now, we are serene in God's grace knowing that he has forgiven our failings of yesterday and has prepared our hearts for this particular moment in time.

We all began our lives as little people full of energy, hope, and vitality. We focused solely on the day and hour we possessed. What happened to our ability to drink of life deeply and to wring the last possible drop of life out of each moment? As I look back on my personal history and consider how I developed into an adult who lost the focus on the now of my life, I think it is a pattern that may be typical—one to which we can all relate. See if your story parallels mine in any way.

As a little girl, I remember dressing my blond-haired doll, eating liverwurst sandwiches for lunch, smelling the snapdragons pretending they would bite my nose, playing with Prince, our big collie dog, roller skating in the driveway, and just "hanging around" with Mary, the next door neighbor. There were hikes, with picnic lunches in brown paper bags, into the woods. Prince would bound along beside us ever vigilant in case we would have trouble finding our way home again. All of those moments were fully lived. We weren't thinking of school starting again in the fall or upcoming Sunday School picnics. Mary, Prince, and I were thinking only of that day's sunshine, roller skates, bagged lunches, and playing house. The moment we owned was all that mattered. If only we could live all of life that way!

TUESDAY

Meditation

"Seek the Lord while he may be found; call on him while he is near."
(Isaiah 55:6)

Spend some time meditating on the emphasis on the present moment in this verse. Ask God to show you the importance of using the time you now own to seek him and to enjoy the life he has given.

Journal

WEDNESDAY

Thoughts for today:

It seems that painful life experiences, coupled with messages from those who seemed to know more about life than I did, worked together to wean me away from the carefree days of living in the present. I remember the day, when I was nine years old, that Prince was hit by a car. We found his bleeding body alongside the road in front of our house. Prince was there, lying still, eyes closed, with low, sad sounds coming from his partially opened mouth. He did not survive.

I had never anticipated that Prince would be taken away from me, so when we were together, I simply loved him and enjoyed him. His death was sudden and was a real shock—one to which I reacted normally: My heart broke for Prince's broken body and for my loss, and I wept inconsolably. That day, I learned that loving included pain, and attachment included separation. To protect myself from experiencing this intense hurt ever again, I would guard the giving of myself in the moment I could control—the now.

Prince was buried lovingly in our back yard. The wooden stick marker served as a reminder of the pain that I would experience if I gave myself fully to the joy, love, and relationship abandoned to the moment. I had already, as a young child, learned to anticipate and protect myself from the future while living in the present.

THURSDAY

Thoughts for today:

All through our lives we have lost much of the depth of present moments and willingness to risk in relationships because of lessons that we interpreted to mean that enjoyment now, if not carefully guarded, could result in pain later. I knew immediately and instinctively at nine years old that if I protected myself from feeling too much in the present moment, I would not feel as much pain when the inevitable loss occurred.

I wish I could have seen then and understood throughout my life that the joy of the moment was worth the pain of the loss. Even the pain of the moment yet to come was worth experiencing to its fullest extent. Each minute of our lives, whatever we are experiencing, is a treasure to be cherished and to be embraced.

God is eternal. He is outside of time. If there is no time to him, he does not think in terms of then and now or past and present or first this and then that. Everything is now—this moment is what eternity is made of. If we are going to become more and more like God, as he has asked us to do, we need to learn more of the eternal perspective, more of the moment-by-moment living that allows us to experience life to its fullest. We need to cherish and live each moment as it presents itself.

FRIDAY

Reading God's message

Ecclesiastes 3:1–11

What is the message of the writer in the first eight verses of this passage? Focus on Verse 11 and put these two phrases in your own words:

"He has made everything beautiful in its time."
"He has also set eternity in the hearts of men."

How does keeping the eternal perspective help you to focus on the present moment?

Journal

SATURDAY

For personal reflection

Think of incidents in your early life that caused you to begin

- to focus on future plans.
- to protect yourself from future pain.
- to regret the past.

What can you do as an adult to spend less time worrying about the future and regretting the past and more time experiencing the present?

How will your life change if you are more involved in the task, the relationship, or the event of the moment?

If that is a change you desire, pray and ask God to change your heart to be in the eternal now with him.

SUNDAY

Prayer

O Father, you are the potter; I am the clay. Help me to be still and let you be God so you can mold me into the image of Christ, the Messiah, the anointed one. My heart desires this. Help my mind to let go of old and false belief systems. Grant me your power in Jesus' holy name.

My prayer:

Cherishing the Moments

P r i n c i p l e   # 25

Fears, worries, and regrets are like clouds that cover the beauty of our lives.

There are things that happen to us in the course of life that initiate in us an instinctive response of self-protection. These defenses keep us from experiencing the exhilarating fullness of the moments in which we live. As we mature, we lose the all-or-nothing approach to life we once had and we become "wiser" and far more careful. Let's examine together the ways in which we have lost our grasp on the present and, by understanding these things, we may be able to clear the cloud cover and begin again to experience life in the fullness that we once did as children.

First, the pain of losing a pet, a friend, or a close relative to an accident or illness causes us to protect ourselves from caring too much in the present moment so we will not feel the pain of loss at a later time. This self-protection has become one of the clouds that we have to clear away if we are ever going to see and experience the now that we want to grasp and know.

Another cloud that obscures the present is that, way too early in our lives, we begin to take on big responsibilities. For example, if we were conscientious students, we felt good about the accolades that came from our early academic successes. Because the feeling was so good, we wanted to excel in school. Therefore, the self-imposed and externally imposed pressure of getting good grades was upon us at a young age. We began the process of preparing for tests, worrying about our performance on them, and anticipating the return of the graded papers. While we were doing all that preparing, worrying, and anticipating, we were losing the present moment which was the only moment we actually could experience in fullness. We developed early the ability to worry about the future!

We have been socialized so thoroughly that the *future, performance, acceptance, and avoidance of pain* far outweigh relishing the moments of which life is made. Every present moment we lost represented the loss of a precious moment of resting in the presence and joy of our Creator.

God is eternal. He neither protects himself from the future nor worries about it. As we learn to know him, we begin to enter into the fullness of now by trusting in his protection and in his willingness to guide our futures one day at a time.

TUESDAY

Meditation

"Desperate, I throw myself on you: You are my God! Hour by hour I place my days in your hand…"
(Psalm 31:14–15 *The Message*)

Meditate on the truths of these verses and then commit this day, this hour, this moment to him. As you do that throughout the day, you will find that you are entering more fully into each moment of your life.

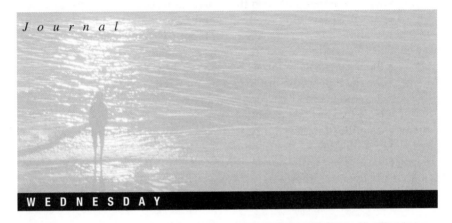

Journal

WEDNESDAY

Thoughts for today:

Another cloud blocking the nowness of our living is *fear*, which began to play a part in our lives as we became more aware of the world around us and as concerned adults began to warn us of strangers, of drowning, of tornadoes, and of a God who would be angry if we did not do everything right. Fear worked together with responsibility to cause us to live in the future instead of in the present. What if a tornado came and blew our house down? What if a bad man chased us on the school playground? What if…? What if…? During all the "what if's" that plagued our lives, the present moment disappeared and the childlike faith in a God who cared and watched over us began to fade.

Then came the part of our lives when *regret* entered the picture: sorrow for and worry about our sins and failures. What if someone found out about the lie we told? What if the teacher humiliated us by reading aloud the note we passed in class? Developing an awareness of sin is not a bad trait for an aspiring young Christian, but our often ineffective way of dealing with our childish sinfulness made us live with regret for the past instead of enjoying constant communion with our heavenly Father who was (and still is!) always willing to hear our confession and forgive our sin.

THURSDAY

T h o u g h t s   f o r   t o d a y :

By the time we were in high school, the aspiring part of our natures caused us to begin to live far into the future: If we had a Christian perspective, we often sought God's will for our lives. That meant we prayed, we read the Bible, we investigated fields of work, we looked at college curricula and catalogs. Those were all good things and yielded some benefits for the very moment. However, the search for God's will also created a future focus that involved trying to do the right thing so that we would succeed.

How much of the moment with those around us did we miss because we were so focused on knowing the future and figuring out God's mysterious will that we would not take a wrong path? If only we had known, as we know now, that all God really wanted from us was

- the willingness to follow him,
- the habit of crying out to him in our need,
- the enjoyment of his presence, and
- trust that he was in control.

Sometimes understanding our past helps us to overcome it. Then, with our relationship with God comfortably in place, the present moment becomes a blessing to be enjoyed with complete confidence that it is given from the hand of a loving heavenly Father who just wants to share it with us!

FRIDAY

R e a d i n g   G o d ' s   m e s s a g e

Psalm 25

As you read this psalm, make notes of these things:
What verses show David's desire to live in the present instead of the past?
What phrases indicate David's trust in God for his future?
Which words show the psalmist's desire to have God lead him?
What do you learn about the attitude we must have if we are to live in present fellowship with God?

J o u r n a l

SATURDAY

For personal reflection

Are you losing the precious moments of life? Ask yourself these questions: What pain am I trying to avoid? What worries do I have about the future? What fears am I harboring? What regrets do I have about the past? Then write your answers below:

_____

_____

_____

As you think about these questions, you may begin to realize how a focus on the past and/or on the future is creating clouds over the present moment so that you cannot see it clearly or experience it fully.

Pray, giving those pains, worries, regrets, and fears to God. Then commit today to pay attention to the life you have in this moment and cherish the clarity that such attention will give to your day.

SUNDAY

Prayer

Lord, help me stay focused on you no matter what happens, seated with you in the heavenlies seeing things and people as you see them—with eyes of love. Never let me stray from your side. Give me your love for obedience to the Father. I praise your holy, powerful name, Jesus.

My prayer:

_____

_____

_____

_____

_____

Clearing the Cloud Cover

P r i n c i p l e # 26

We would be fools to focus only on the present moment if we did not believe that someone wiser and stronger than we are is in charge of our lives.

As we look back on our lives, we have to think that God would be more pleased if we had cherished each moment and had allowed him to lead us one step at a time instead of our spending so much precious time looking for the magical roadmap that would lead to blessing and pleasure instead of pain and sorrow. Our regret for the past, fear of failure, and constant searching for future direction have caused us to lose the joy and experience of too many of the present moments of our lives.

For a God who is eternal, there is no past or future; there is only the eternal *now*. And for much of our lives we have missed it. We don't want to miss it any longer. We need to relearn how to live our lives, how to let go of regretting the past or being controlled by it, and how to trust the God of our future to unfold it one day at a time so that the future is not anticipated, just lived out in fullness moment by moment.

Jesus taught his disciples that they were like sheep and he was the shepherd who cared for them, looked out for their needs, rescued them, fed them, and made them feel secure and loved. Jesus said that all his sheep had to do was to "go in and out and find pasture." These sheep didn't have a worry in the world. They knew that the shepherd loved them enough to give his own life, if necessary, to keep them safe.

As Sheldon Van Auken says in his book *The Severe Mercy*, "Sometimes— more precisely, some-not-times—we find 'the still point of the turning world'. All our most lovely moments perhaps are timeless" (HarperCollins Publishers, Inc., 1980, p. 201).

How can we experience the lovely, timeless moments Van Auken describes? How can we go about recapturing the essence of the *now* that we had as fresh-from-eternity children and somehow lost along the way? We will look at some simple concepts that may help us in the process of recapturing the simple, present-moment lives we have lost.

To begin capturing the now, we must entrust ourselves fully to God. It is only then that we will feel safe enough to live in the present moment without worrying about the future or regretting the past. We have already learned a lot about trust in our journey together. Now we need to carry the concept over into present-moment living.

T U E S D A Y

M e d i t a t i o n

"We who have run for our very lives to God have every reason to grab the promised hope with both hands and never let go. It's an unbreakable spiritual lifeline, reaching past all appearances right to the very presence of God ... ."
(Hebrews 6:18–19 *The Message*)

Meditate on these verses, focusing on what it means to be in the very presence of God.

J o u r n a l

W E D N E S D A Y

T h o u g h t s   f o r   t o d a y :

In order to live in the present moment, we have to free ourselves of the past and of the future. If the past haunts us, we must take care of it by confessing to God what we feel guilty about. If God leads us to go to another person to make apologies or restitution, we must do that, too. If we need healing from past hurts that others have inflicted upon us, we need to ask for God's healing touch. If the pains of the past are deep, and if we have lived with them for a long time, we may have to go through this process over a period of time until we really sense God's forgiveness, his healing, and his restorative power. It will happen; we must not give up until it does.

Then we can give him our future, too. When we, in constant prayer throughout the day, give him our attention and our very selves, long-range goals don't seem as important anymore. Our future doesn't seem as frightening or as demanding. God removes our fear and fills our hearts with peace and with assurance that he is in control as long as we allow him to be. He knows the future and we don't. Why would we worry about something for which our loving and all-powerful heavenly Father already has the answer?

THURSDAY

Thoughts for today:

If we allow God to cleanse and heal our past and if we trust him with our future, does that mean we will not have any problems to face? No, but it does mean that we will not face them until they happen. There will be no reason to worry about them ahead of time, to plan for them, to think about how we will deal with them, or to wish them away.

I am reminded of the instructions that Jesus gave to his disciples when he was telling them that they would be persecuted after he left. He said to them, "But when they arrest you, do not worry about what to say or how to say it. At that time you will be given what to say, for it will not be you speaking, but the Spirit of your Father speaking through you" (Matthew 10:19–20). When I think of the number of rehearsed speeches I have presented to my steering wheel on my way to meetings, I realize all of the present moments I have wasted in anticipation of what I would need to say or do. That is not how Jesus told his disciples to live.

We are the sheep of his fold of whom Jesus said, "I have come that they may have life, and have it to the full" (John 10:10b). Fullness of life means relishing every moment of it beginning right now!

FRIDAY

Reading God's message

Luke 12:22–40

What kinds of things does Jesus tell us not to worry about? Why does he say it is futile to worry? What reassurance does he give that such worry is not necessary? What should we do instead of worrying? Is there an application of these principles that you can make in your own life?

Journal

SATURDAY

For personal reflection

Are you ready to let God renew you and make your character more like his eternal nature? If so, tell him. Yield today to him and request these things:

Show me what I need to see in each moment of today.

Allow me to feel the emotions that each moment opens up.

Free me of concerns and distractions from the present moment.

Remind me over and over again today of your presence in the nows of my life.

Write down anything that comes to your mind as you pray these prayers. What do you need to change in the way you live your life in order to experience the fullness of each moment?

_____

_____

SUNDAY

Prayer

Lord, you have come to free me from the tyranny of myself. Break the taskmaster mentality in me and let me see and personally involve myself in your calm and pleasant presence in this moment. I will choose to gaze into your eyes and receive your love.

My prayer:

_____

_____

_____

_____

_____

Trusting God for the Now

105

P r i n c i p l e # 27

If we think that God doesn't like to have fun, we have never really looked at a duck-billed platypus.

To live in the present moment we have to let go of both the past and the future. We must be forgiven and healed of issues in our past, and we must stop worrying about the future. When we really quit anticipating the future and the problems it may bring, we are able to live in the present moment and then, when difficult life situations come, we can deal with them at that time and, perhaps, even enjoy the challenge of meeting them head on with the God of the universe leading the charge. This is what the life of faith is all about—faith in God's loving care and in his ability to see and prepare for the future and to take care of the past better than we can.

There was a time when my two daughters taught me the lesson of fully enjoying and entering into the joy of the now. We had gone to an amusement park together and, while they were very excited about a particular roller coaster in which passengers were whirled upside-down, I was not too enthused about it. But, as their mom, I needed to be a good sport, so I said I would go on the ride. As we stood in line, I dreaded getting into the car and eventually being propelled through the roller coaster maze. But, by sheer willpower, I made it through and mentally patted myself on the back for my bravery.

As the car came to a stop and we clambered out, my older daughter, Andrea, said, "Wasn't it cool to watch the trees go by as we went upside down?" I grinned and admitted sheepishly, "I don't know. I had my eyes closed." You see, I was enduring the present moment—not enjoying it!

Her immediate response was not what I wanted to hear, "Then we have to go again. And this time you need to keep your eyes open!" I found myself in line once more for the ride of my life (This, by the way, is the last roller coaster ride I plan to experience in this lifetime—unless my grandchildren are terribly persuasive!). This time, I kept my eyes open. This time, I let myself get more fully into the experience—and into the sheer terror I felt.

Were it not for my girls, I would have gone through this important life experience without fully entering into it! Sometimes we have to let go in order to experience the moments that God has given.

TUESDAY

Meditation

"I came so they can have real and eternal life, more and better life than they ever dreamed of."
(John 10:10b *The Message*)

Let's take time today to really think about the significance of this verse. Meditate today on what your life would look like if you experienced the fullness of every moment. What does "more and better life" mean to you?

Journal

WEDNESDAY

Thoughts for today:

Jesus describes himself as as the good shepherd. As our shepherd he says, "I know my sheep and my sheep know me" (John 10:14). He knows what makes us happy. He knows how to pet us, how to nurture us, and how to provide the very best of life's pleasures for us. And he knows how to play with us.

One of the things we discover, once we are free of the baggage of the past and the future, is that life is really a lot more fun than we ever thought it could be. We will never be able to have fun if we are haunted by the past or if we are living only for the future. Once we have given both our history and our life to come over to God and have placed our trust firmly in him, we will be able to kick up our heels and allow ourselves to enjoy the time that is in our grasp right now. And God is right there beside us enjoying us as we enjoy the gift of life he has given.

We need not look forward to the day when things will be better, we will have more money, or people will be nicer. We need not look at the past and remember the "good ol' days." The present moment is what we have. We don't want to waste it. We want to live it.

THURSDAY

Thoughts for today:

God does not live in the past, nor does he want us to. We cannot remake old decisions or undo past actions. God does not live in the future. He knows what will happen and, in his sovereignty, he engineers what he chooses in order to create his purposes in this world and in our lives. For God there is only the present.

God wants to enjoy us and to relate to us in a way that is full of praise, love, mercy, compassion, and satisfaction. For example, here are a few verses from Psalm 103: "Praise the Lord, O my soul, and forget not all His benefits—Who forgives all your sins and heals all your diseases, who redeems your life from the pit and crowns you with love and compassion, who satisfies your desires with good things so that your youth is renewed like the eagle's."

All of this is in the present. Right now we are to be praising God, acknowledging his blessings, and accepting his forgiveness and healing. He is redeeming us, satisfying us, renewing us. As a result we have, right now, love, compassion, good things, satisfied desires, and renewed youth.

This is true joy, and all of it is in the present moment. We cannot borrow these gifts from the future or insert them into the past. We just need to accept and to enjoy them *now*!

FRIDAY

Reading God's message

Psalm 68:3–4; Proverbs 5:18; Romans 12:15; Philippians 4:4; James 1:2

Read each of these verses and write beside each one in the journal space below what kinds of things God wants us to enjoy:

Journal

Psalm 68:3–4

Proverbs 5:18

Romans 12:15

Philippians 4:4

James 1:2

SATURDAY

For personal reflection

Think outside the box and figure out what you can do today just for fun. Then do it!

Share the fun with a friend, a family member, or your spouse if you want to. Or share your fun with God alone.

Ask God to show you how to enjoy, really enjoy, the moments of this earthly life. Fun fits in the tiniest of places! Find spots for it throughout your day.

Write here what you did, just for fun:

_____

_____

_____

SUNDAY

Prayer

Father, kind Father, when I refuse to join the circle of your fun-loving people, show me how much I am robbing myself. Help me to relax and enjoy. Give me grace to abandon myself to you fully and completely. It is what we both want. In Jesus' name. Amen.

My prayer:

_____

_____

_____

_____

_____

Be Prepared to Have Fun

P r i n c i p l e # 28

We don't want to get to the end of our lives and find out that we missed living!

Living in the present moment will require some discipline because we have deeply ingrained habits that need to be broken in order to allow us to capture the now. There are some tools that can help us do this if we practice putting them to work. For example, when we are in conversation with someone, we must focus, with as much attention as we can muster, on what the person is saying and what he/she is trying to communicate. This *focused attention* is given instead of thinking about what we are going to say next or wondering what we should fix for dinner.

Another tool is becoming *more and more aware of our five senses*. What are we seeing right now? We must see it in detail. What do we hear? Let's begin to listen to all the sounds that we have tuned out through the years. What does the steering wheel or garden soil feel like under our fingertips? Is the air around us warm, cold, stale, or fresh? When we block out our senses, we skim over the present moment and don't experience its fullness. There will never be again the combination of sensory input that each of us is experiencing right now. We want to feel it, see it, hear it, take it all in.

Emotional awareness is important, too. Periodically throughout the day we should ask ourselves, "What am I feeling right now?" Are there negative thoughts running through our heads? If they are valid, we must deal with them. If they are not, we should consciously dismiss them. We do emotional check-ins not to shut down what we do not want to feel, but to enter into and fully experience the feelings that we are having. How else can we be ourselves to the fullest? How else can we really be living in the present moment?

A *spiritual awareness* is perhaps the most important part of the present moment. As we remind ourselves to direct our attention to God, at least for that moment we are attuned to the eternality of the present, we are communicating with God, and we are living with awareness of the preciousness of this moment of life.

Now is the only time that matters. The most necessary thing we have to do is in front of us right now. The most important person we have to deal with is with us in this moment. The good deed or kind word that we want to say needs to be done, or said *now*.

TUESDAY

Meditation

"Your life is a journey you must travel with a deep consciousness of God."
(I Peter 1:17b *The Message*)

Ponder these words. What is God's message to you about what it means to have a deep consciousness of him? Ask him to show you. Write down what he needs.

Journal

WEDNESDAY

Thoughts for today:

One effective tool in maintaining a continual, present moment connection with God is to adopt a reminder phrase. For example, before we enter a room, go into a store, or walk into a meeting, we may say quietly to ourselves, "Hallowed be thy name." This reminds us that our underlying desire, in that moment and in that place, is for God's name to be glorified.

Other similar God-reminders that have been adopted by people through the years include, "Thine alone" or "Holy, holy, holy." As we whisper these phrases to ourselves throughout the day, we are reminded we are living in the eternal *now* of God's presence and of his perfect timing for every event and relationship in our lives.

Another way of experiencing the joy of living in the moment is to cultivate a thankful heart. Psalm 103, which we looked at together earlier, opens with praise—praise from the soul, praise from "my inmost being" and remembering with thanksgiving all the benefits that God has given. A thankful heart will focus on the present moment and on the blessings from God's hand that we experience right now. God doesn't want us to forget what he has done in the past, but only to the extent that remembering the past helps us to trust him more while we enjoy and are thankful for the *now*.

THURSDAY

Thoughts for today:

Let's agree that we will seek intentional now-focused living beginning with the moment we have now. As we recount our own life histories, I think we will find that our lives begin with simple living; but as we learn what is expected in our world and in our culture, they begin to get more and more complex. We find ourselves living in the past or living for tomorrow or even for the next hour and losing the only time when we have any power to make a difference in the world in which we live.

We have already acknowledged that we need to be willing to unlearn some patterns we have picked up in our lives and, through discipline and with confidence, relearn how to capture this very moment, to live it, enjoy it, use it and be used in it, and to be thankful for everything that it contains.

We don't want to miss real life by missing the *nows* that comprise it. Let's commit that we will simply grab onto the moment and let ourselves grin while we enjoy the ride! And we will keep our eyes open the entire time! While it may sound trite, we all know that it is true that this very moment is all that we have. Don't waste it. Don't lose it. And, for heaven's sake (and yours), don't *miss* it!

FRIDAY

Reading God's message

II Corinthians 5:14–6:2

Read this passage, listing the ways in which Paul's directives to the Corinthians involve changes in their daily lives. In *The Message*, II Corinthians 6:1b reads, "...please don't squander one bit of this marvelous life God has given us." How do the words of Paul in this passage help us understand how to live life fully, as God intended?

Journal

SATURDAY

For personal reflection

Choose right now a phrase or a word that will remind you of God's presence in your life. You may have your own idea, but if you need suggestions, here are some choices:

Hallowed be thy name	Holy, Holy, Holy	Thine alone
O Lord, My God	You are worthy	Yours, Lord

Begin to practice saying it. Write it on sticky notes and put it on your mirror, on your dashboard, on your calendar, and, yes, on your television.

Practice God's presence in the present moment by reminding yourself that he is there.

Breathe a prayer of commitment to him every time you remember him.

At the end of the day, evaluate and see if acknowledging God made a difference in your attitude and in your focus on the present moment.

SUNDAY

Prayer

Lord, you tell me that if I take the time, you will show me beauty every day—and you do! You are a beautiful Savior and you give us the blessed hope of living with you forever. We receive this hope and renew it in every moment of our lives. Thank you!

My prayer:

_____

_____

_____

_____

_____

A Time to Live

WEEK
TWENTY-NINE

Living by Faith

MONDAY

P r i n c i p l e   # 29

Living by faith is as unnatural to humans as swimming under water.

It is interesting to follow the events that occur when the cardinals convene at the Vatican to elect a new Pope. The crowds are outside in St. Peter's Square watching the chimney for the white smoke to appear which will indicate that a new Pope has been elected.

After God's leadership is sought, votes are taken by the cardinals that eventually result in the election of a new leader of the Roman Catholic Church. But the matter is not complete simply by counting the votes. The next step is crucial as the Pope-elect approaches the front of the Sistine Chapel and the head of the College of Cardinals looks into his face and asks, "Do you accept the election?" If the cardinal believes that God has chosen him for this role, he accepts, in faith, his new appointment. White smoke, at last, billows from the chimney and there is great rejoicing among the crowds gathered in St. Peter's Square.

"Do you accept the election?" This is a question that all of us have to answer! God chooses us to be part of his eternal kingdom, but he looks each one of us in the face and asks, "Do you accept the election?" We are fully aware, as is the cardinal now elected as Pope, that we are not able to earn the honor of this new appointment. Therefore, the only way we can accept the election is to do so in faith, believing in the God who has chosen us. When we declare our acceptance, white smoke comes forth from the celestial chimney and, the Bible tells us, there is great rejoicing among the angels in heaven.

We can understand what faith is all about when it comes to our salvation. We know we cannot earn our way into relationship with God; so, in faith, we accept the plan that God has offered; we accept the payment that Jesus has made through his death on the cross and his resurrection three days later. There is the feeling of "Whew! I'm in!" We exercised the faith that our salvation calls for mostly because it was really clear to us that we had no other choice. We could not measure up on our own; we had proved that by failing so many times already. We were cornered. We had no choice but to reach out in faith to the God who said he would save us if we called on his name. It is clear that beginning our life with God requires faith. But, then what?

114

TUESDAY

Meditation

"Just go ahead with what you've been given. You received Christ Jesus, the Master; now live him. You're deeply rooted in him. You're well constructed upon him. You know your way around the faith. Now do what you've been taught. School's out; quit studying the subject and start living it! And let your living spill over into thanksgiving."
(Colossians 2:6 *The Message*)

Read this verse carefully and then allow God to direct your meditation to one phrase. Focus on those words only and allow the Holy Spirit to speak to you.

Journal

WEDNESDAY

Thoughts for today:

For many of us, who now call ourselves believers, our faith gets put back on the shelf at the point of acceptance of Christ as Savior. Instead of living by faith, we fall back into old patterns of trying to measure up. That is not what God intended. His direction throughout Scripture, especially in New Testament writings, is that our entire life must be lived by faith. We need to understand that instruction and apply it to our walk even after conversion. The Christian life can be nothing less than a faith-driven life, but living by faith is a decision we have to make day by day.

Once we become Christians, we must not fall back on the old ways of trying to earn our own way. Instead, we must learn to:

- believe the promises of God's word,
- rest in the assurances of his love,
- listen for his guidance, and
- live by faith.

The faith life will not happen naturally. Faith is a gift that God gives us; it is not natural, but supernatural; it is not humanly contrived, but spiritually endowed. Living by faith is as unnatural to humans as swimming under water, but once God enlivens us spiritually, it is as if we have grown gills and, over time, our faith life becomes so natural we become as fish swimming happily in the glorious freedom of clear, blue waters.

THURSDAY

Thoughts for today:

Living by faith involves breaking all kinds of old habits. We are used to getting paychecks for the work we performed. We are used to having dessert because we cleaned our plates. We are accustomed to receiving praise for leading the Bible study at church. If we don't produce, we don't receive the rewards; if we do produce, we think we merit recognition. In God's kingdom it doesn't work that way. We live by faith. We don't have to *do* anything to gain God's approval except to trust him.

The Bible uses Abraham as an illustration of a man of faith. James tells us that Abraham's faith, not his action, was credited to him as righteousness. Abraham trusted God and did things in obedience to God, but Abraham's actions were not done to earn God's favor. He already had God's approval just because of his faith.

We can serve God to gain approval points or we can serve God because the service flows out of our faith walk with him. The point-earning actions will be frustrating to us and unproductive in God's kingdom even though we might receive approval from folks around us who observe our hard work. The service that we give which grows out of our faith-walk will be empowered by God, and he will receive all the glory from the results of our work. We know which of the two we would rather have!

FRIDAY

Reading God's message

Romans 4

As you read this chapter, make a list of the ways in which Abraham was obedient to God. What attitude preceded his obedience? According to this passage, how are we justified? What does not justify us in God's sight? What does the term *justification* mean to you?

Journal

SATURDAY

For   personal   reflection

Evaluate the many tasks and goals you are juggling in your life right now. Write down the top three.

Which of these are you doing entirely by faith?

Which are you doing because you think you have the ability or the responsibility to do so and you will work really hard until you get it right?

How is your attitude different if you are doing something because you have faith that God is working through you versus if you are doing something because you think you can figure it out and accomplish it on your own?

Which attitude would you rather live with?

Begin to put faith into practice in every area of your life and at every hour of the day.

SUNDAY

Prayer

Lord, you invite me into your full power and authority. Would you show me what keeps me from appropriating it into my life? Give me the humility to receive from you since you resist the proud and give grace to the humble. I ask this in Jesus' name. Amen.

My prayer:

_____

_____

_____

_____

_____

Living by Faith

P r i n c i p l e   # 30

We don't have to be perfect, we just have to be his.

God has promised that he will conform us to the image of Jesus. Because we are goal-oriented people, we tend to think that we can move that process along and reach that perfection sooner rather than later. After all, wouldn't our perfection please God? He should be happy that we are so eager to get on with it. The problem is that, as frail human beings, we try and fail, and then get discouraged. Eventually we give up.

Brother Lawrence was a seventeenth-century French layman who gave himself in service as a kitchen worker at a Carmelite monastery in Paris. He is best known for a little book of his letters and sayings in which he expresses his one desire, which was to live in constant awareness of God and in continual communion with him.

You would think that such a devoted follower of God would never sin. But that is not the case. Brother Lawrence was very aware of his sinfulness. Then you would think that when he did fall into sin, he would berate himself, bemoan his humanity, and cast himself in abject hopelessness upon the mercy of God. He did see the need to ask for forgiveness. And he did understand the severity of his sin. But he also understood God's willingness and ability to forgive.

This is what a monk who wrote about Brother Lawrence said about his confession of sin: "That he was very sensible of his faults, but not discouraged by them; that he confessed them to God, but did not plead against him to excuse them. When he had so done, he peaceably resumed his usual practice of love and adoration" (Spire Books, 1967, p. 32). The great faith he had was borne of his close relationship with God and enabled him to take God at his word and accept the forgiveness that is so freely offered to all of us who are his.

It takes faith to believe God when he says he loves us, forgives us, and restores our relationship when we come to him in sincere confession. We must not despair that we are not yet purified of sin. Sin is part of the human condition. Instead we exercise faith as we approach the God who loves us in spite of our imperfection. Our trust and our obedience are what He is looking for, not our perfect walk. Think of the joy we will know working in partnership with God, who accepts us just as we are!

TUESDAY

Meditation

"God, I'm not trying to rule the roost,
I don't want to be king of the mountain.
I haven't meddled where I have no business or fantasized grandiose plans.
I've kept my feet on the ground, I've cultivated a quiet heart.
Like a baby content in its mother's arms, my soul is a baby content."
(Psalm 131:1–2 *The Message*)

Meditate on this psalm and what it teaches us about ending the struggle to be better and better and, instead, resting by faith in God's arms. Allow God to lead you to a portion of this Scripture that speaks to *your* need.

Journal

WEDNESDAY

Thoughts for today:

The life of faith frees us from having to be perfect. We already know that we cannot reach perfection. Now is the time to quit trying! In what ways do we get caught up in the perfection trap?

First we go about trying to eliminate sin from our lives. God wants us to be holy and righteous. But that holiness will come from him as we walk daily in his presence. Even when we are trying our very best, we will fail. That failure does not take God by surprise. He knows that we are frail and prone to sin, so he has made provision for our fallenness. If we confess our sins, we receive God's forgiveness, and are restored to fellowship and service. By an act of our wills, we accept in faith that God is faithful to his promise to forgive and cleanse. Then we move on.

But what if we fall into the same sin again? Surely at that point, God is angry? No. He still invites us with open arms to come back to him, dirt and all, to confess our failure, and allow him to clean us up and set us on the right path again. After awhile, as we grow in our spiritual awareness, the allure of sin will become less and less, but while God is perfecting us, he simply wants us to accept by faith that he is ready and willing to forgive.

THURSDAY

Thoughts for today:

Living by faith will eliminate unhealthy perfectionism from our lives. We have all heard, "If a job is worth doing, it's worth doing well!" If we accepted that statement as children, we may now have the mindset that if we can't perform a task perfectly, we should not do it at all. So we learn to avoid new challenges or we procrastinate until the last possible moment before tackling a difficult task. This attitude is not one that is God-focused. It is self-focused and self-dependent. And it keeps us from even attempting to do some things that may enrich our lives and the lives of those around us.

God doesn't expect perfection of us! He just wants us to be obedient to whatever task he sets in front of us. We do so trusting that, if we are living by faith, the job will be completed according to his standards and not ours. Remember that our definition of a successful job and God's may differ greatly. Sometimes he is most glorified in what, from a human perspective, feels like a failed endeavor. And sometimes he empowers us to do far greater things than we ever thought we could.

If we throw away the attitude of perfectionism and trust him for the outcome of our efforts, the work will be profitable for God's kingdom and we will know that what was accomplished was God's doing and not our own.

FRIDAY

Reading God's message

I John 1:1–2:2

What does this passage tell you about God's willingness to forgive? What does it tell you about how to receive that forgiveness? What do you learn from these verses about Jesus' role in our being forgiven? What does it mean to you to have fellowship with God, the Father? With Jesus?

Journal

SATURDAY

For personal reflection

What job are you putting off because you are afraid you cannot do it perfectly?

_____

_____

What new skill do you secretly want to learn but you know others are better at it than you are?

_____

What person might you be willing to talk to about spiritual issues, but you're afraid you don't have all the answers?

_____

If God is asking you to do something, commit the task to him, and then begin trusting that he will work in and through you to make your work usable for his kingdom even though your efforts may not reach perfection in your eyes.

SUNDAY

Prayer

Lord Jesus, I need your constant assurance that I am your child and that you love me no matter what. I need your constant assurance that I can never be separated from you; you are my confidence and my courage to keep growing and changing. Thank you that I can never wear you out with my coming. You are glorious!

My prayer:

_____

_____

_____

_____

The Faith Life Allows Imperfection

The Faith Life Is Free of Guilt and Anxiety

P r i n c i p l e   # 31

God breathes peace into my soul.

If we really trust God to treat us the way he says he will, we never have to live with either guilt or anxiety again. He has promised to clean up our sinfulness and he has promised to replace our anxiety with peace.

Will we ever sin? Yes. We know that we will and so does God. But when we do, we will be aware of it (the Holy Spirit has promised to convict us) and we will go to him in faith believing that he will forgive us, cleanse us, and renew our relationship with him. I John 1:9 says, "If we confess our sins, he is faithful and just and will forgive us our sins and purify us from all unrighteousness." In *The Message*, that verse reads, "If we admit our sins—make a clean breast of them—he won't let us down; he'll be true to himself. He'll forgive our sins and purge us of all wrongdoing." He not only forgives the sins we know about and confess, but when we confess what we know to be wrong, he goes a step further and cleans us up from *all* unrighteousness.

If we accept this verse in faith, why would we ever leave the throne of God carrying guilt? If we do, it is because we have not believed him when he said he would forgive. Or it is because Satan comes around with his guilt, which he knows will cripple our relationship with God. Satan would rather have us feel bad about ourselves and our sinfulness than to have us experience God's forgiveness.

Faith is required, however, to overcome our own tenacity in hanging on to guilt. Sometimes I think it makes us feel more spiritual when we acknowledge the great degree of our sinfulness! Yes, we are sinful and deserve punishment. But God said that, through Jesus, sin has been taken care of. We can choose to believe him or we can revert to our own version of our unworthiness. After all, can we expect God to forgive us again and again for the same sin? Yes. If he says he will forgive us when we confess, he will. If we accept God's promises in faith, we confess every time we fall into sin. He forgives and cleanses. That is his nature. That is what he does. That's what Jesus died to do. God made this promise and is true to his word.

TUESDAY

Meditation

**"If you, God, kept records on wrongdoings,
who would stand a chance?
As it turns out, forgiveness is your habit,
And that's why you're worshiped."**
(Psalm 130:3–4 *The Message*)

Meditate on these verses. Then spend some time in worship of the God who has made forgiveness a habit!

Journal

WEDNESDAY

Thoughts for today:

After confession, we can enjoy the feeling of being clean and then we go back to God with a grateful heart for all of his mercy and grace. If we live by faith we don't ever live with guilt. We are free of that burden!

Not only can we live guilt-free lives, we don't have to worry anymore either. Living a worry-free life is really very simple if we take God at his word. Philippians 4:6 (*The Message*) says, "Don't fret or worry. Instead of worrying, pray. Let petitions and praises shape your worries into prayers, letting God know your concerns. Before you know it, a sense of God's wholeness, everything coming together for good, will come and settle you down. It's wonderful what happens when Christ displaces worry at the center of your life."

We have a promise here. If we turn our anxieties into prayers, God will give us, in turn, a sense of wholeness, a calmness—the New International Version of the Bible calls it the "peace of God which transcends all understanding" (Phil 4:7).

Now, how do we get something so great that we can't understand it? We can't get it by studying it, by earning it, or by buying it. It is a gift that we can receive only by faith. We simply must decide to believe that God will do what he says he will do.

THURSDAY

Thoughts for today:

No matter how closely we walk with God, there are things that come into our lives that will steal our peace. When that happens and we turn, sometimes desperately, to God, we will find that he comes in his very quiet way and says, "Just tell me about all of the things that are troubling you." With that invitation, we begin to pray—not even with a lot of faith—that the promised calmness will, in fact, overtake us. We need to believe what God says, obey him even if it doesn't seem logical to do so, and trust him to bring about the results he has promised. When we do those things, peace will rule our hearts.

As we observe people around us, we can tell that many long for lives free of the stresses that plague them, lives full of the peace that now eludes them. Jesus promises *rest* to his followers. God promises *peace* to those who take their anxieties to him in prayer. Imagine a life free of anxiety, free of worry, and free of stress. A life like that can be ours; we just need to listen to what God says about giving our worries over to him, communicate our concerns to him in prayer, and then, in faith, accept and relish the supernatural peace that he has promised to give.

FRIDAY

Reading God's message

Colossians 1:1–20

Paul is thankful for the Colossian believers. What specifically does he thank God for? What does Paul pray that God will do for these Christians? What does he say their lives should look like? How does he describe Jesus in Verses 15–20? Verse 20 in *The Message* reads as follows: "All the broken and dislocated pieces of the universe—people and things, animals and atoms—get properly fixed and fit together in vibrant harmonies, all because of his death, his blood that poured down from the cross." What does Verse 20 tell us about what Jesus has done to bring peace to us and to the world?

Journal

SATURDAY

For   personal   reflection

For what sins do you need to be forgiven?

_____

Simply and honestly confess those sins to God and, in faith, accept the forgiveness that he so freely offers. Thank him for the freedom from guilt that you experience, and then begin to live in faith knowing that there is nothing blocking your relationship with your heavenly Father.

What are you stressed out about today? What anxieties do you carry?

_____

Turn them, one-by-one, into prayers and allow the peace of God to fill your heart. Give him thanks. Then go through your day believing that the peace he has given you will rule in your life.

SUNDAY

Prayer

Put flesh on your instructions, Lord, to be still and know that you are God. That is all I need to walk through my day in confidence and joy. Let this word renew my mind to know you better and follow you more closely. I ask in the awesome name of Jesus. Amen.

My prayer:

_____

_____

_____

_____

The Faith Life Is Free of Guilt and Anxiety

P r i n c i p l e   # 32

We can know with confidence that we will become what God has always had in mind for us to be.

If we live in our own strength, we give a great deal of time and energy to pleasing other people. We are concerned about what people think of us, how we look, whether we get credit for the job we did, and not offending anyone.

If we live by faith, all of that disappears because we now have only one person to please and that is God himself. Not only that, but God has already declared us to be acceptable in his sight through the blood of his son, Jesus.

What results from that total acceptance by God and the disappearance of the need to please others? We can be free to be ourselves and to live with a new confidence and boldness. In doing so, we find that people actually like us better and respect us more. The people we once tried so hard to please now respond in a new and better way to us. And God is our cheerleader, urging us to be all that we can be in relationship to him.

Do you remember Jesus' disciple, Peter?

He was the one who walked on the water to Jesus and then nearly drowned when he began to get distracted by the waves around him. He was the one who in one breath acknowledged that Jesus was the promised Messiah and in the next argued with Jesus saying that the things Jesus was telling his disciples about his coming death were not true. As if Jesus would lie! Peter was the one who impetuously cut off the ear of the soldier when Jesus' captors came to arrest him in the Garden of Gethsemane. Jesus had to put the ear back on and heal it! He was the one who vowed he would never deny Jesus and would, in fact, die with him if necessary. Then, that very night, he denied three times that he ever knew his Lord.

Peter was the apostle who just didn't seem to understand the life of faith during the time that he was one of Jesus' most vocal and unpredictable of disciples. But we find by reading his later writings that, throughout his lifetime, he learned a lot about trusting God. We know what Peter was when Jesus met him; let's look together at what he became over a lifetime of walking with his Lord. Seeing Peter's transformation will give us hope, too! God is in the business of changing us into people of confidence and joy.

TUESDAY

Meditation

"I want you woven into a tapestry of love, in touch with everything there is to know of God. Then you will have minds confident and at rest, focused on Christ, God's great mystery."
(Colossians 2:2 *The Message*)

Ponder what God is saying to you through this verse in his word. What does it mean to be in touch with everything there is to know of God? Or to have minds confident and at rest?

Journal

WEDNESDAY

Thoughts   for   today:

By the time he was nearing the end of his life, Peter wrote about living the confident life of faith. As we read through his two letters, written when he was older and wiser than he was when he was following Jesus around Galilee, we find descriptions of just what we would want our Christian lives to look like. We realize that the confident life we seek will come only through faith just as it did for Peter. He could not bring this transformation about by his own efforts and neither can we. Let's look at some of the insights Peter shares in the first epistle that bears his name.

1 Peter 4:3	...live out your days free to pursue what God wants instead of being tyrannized by what you want. (*The Message*)
1 Peter 4:7–11	...be clear minded and self controlled so that you can pray. Above all, love each other deeply.... (NIV)
1 Peter 5:6	So be content with who you are...God's strong hand is on you; he'll promote you at the right time. (*The Message*)

Do you see the confidence that Peter shows? Throughout this letter, he talks of hope, respect, freedom, self control, prayer, contentment, faithfulness, and love. This is not the Peter we first meet in Scripture. God had changed him into what Jesus knew all along that he could become.

THURSDAY

Thoughts for today:

When Jesus first met Simon, he changed his name. Jesus said that he would no longer be called Simon, but would be called Peter which means *a stone*. When we observe Peter's early relationship with Jesus, he was unstable, changing, emotional, and unpredictable. He was not a stone. Jesus, though, saw the Peter who he would become by faith. Years later, Peter sums his transformation up by saying, "Everything that goes into a life of pleasing God has been miraculously given to us by getting to know, personally and intimately, the One who invited us to God" (II Peter 1:3, *The Message*).

There is something inside us that longs to become the confident man of God Peter had become. There is a security, a peace, a contentment that draws us. How can we achieve such a life? Only by faith. We have to claim God's divine power, believe that he cares for us, that he gives us spiritual gifts for serving, that he hears us when we pray, and that he has a new name for us which reflects the outcome of his work in our lives. We accept these truths simply because God says they are true. Exercising faith in these matters is just exactly the same as exercising our faith in accepting Jesus as Savior. We must simply believe, act on that belief, and then watch as our lives grow in confidence and security.

FRIDAY

Reading God's message

Hebrews 13:1–21

Make a list of all of the commands in this chapter. Then look at Verses 20 and 21 and write in your own words how we are made able to keep all the instructions we are given.

Journal

SATURDAY

For personal reflection

If you have been a Christian for some time now, look back on your spiritual journey and take note of growth you have experienced.

_____

_____

Thank God for changing you more and more into what he has in mind for you to be as you continue your walk with him in faith.

If you are a new Christian, think of ways that God is working in your life right now to bring you closer to him and to mold you into a beautiful, confident child of his.

_____

_____

SUNDAY

Prayer

Increase my faith, Lord, to believe that you mean what you say. Quiet the inner dialogue that doubts and questions. Let me hear you say, "Only believe." I will trust and not be afraid. Empower me, Holy Spirit, as I ask in Jesus' name. Amen.

My prayer:

_____

_____

_____

_____

_____

The Faith Life Is Lived with Confidence

P r i n c i p l e   # 33

Hope is the light that keeps us moving forward even when we are walking through darkness and desperation.

Unless we live in faith, we are unable to live the life that God has designed for us. God gives great promises of working on our behalf, of his power to transform us, of his provision of our needs, and of his desire to engift us for service to him. These promises can be real in our lives only when we accept them by faith.

The story of Martin Luther is a classic example of despair turned to hope and joy when faith entered the picture. We think of Luther as a strong leader who confronted injustices and wrote hymns, but maybe we don't know the rest of the story. Luther's life was plagued by doubt and guilt. He joined a monastery in an effort to live a spiritual life that was pleasing to God. Luther observed the holiness of God, yet he felt overwhelming guilt every day because of his inability to meet God's standards. So he went to confession over and over again. It is said that one day he spent six hours in the confessional listing sins that he had committed just since confession the day before.

Did he live the serene, fulfilling life we aspire to? No. Was it free of anxiety? No. Was it filled with hope? No. Was it free of guilt? No. What was missing from Martin Luther's life of commitment? The answer is simple: Faith. The radical change in Luther's life came when he began to study the book of Romans. He read and understood in his soul the verse that states that the righteous (or the just) shall live by faith. Luther's life changed from that moment on and, instead of wallowing in guilt, penance, and despair, he began to live by faith and to experience God's grace and love. As a result, he grew in spiritual stature to the theological leader that we have come to respect. Luther found that faith is the door to God's grace, forgiveness, peace, and guidance. When we believe the promises and the faithfulness of the one who is trustworthy, radical changes will result: We will be free of guilt, perfectionism, and anxiety and, instead, will be filled with confidence and hope. The circumstances we find ourselves in right now are only precursors to fabulous things to come in this life and in the life hereafter. Therefore we can joyfully anticipate in faith and hope that which God has promised.

TUESDAY

Meditation

"We find ourselves standing where we always hoped we might stand—out in the wide open spaces of God's grace and glory, standing tall and shouting our praise."
(Romans 5:2 *The Message*)

Meditate on this verse and allow the Holy Spirit to minister hope to your heart.

Journal

WEDNESDAY

Thoughts for today:

"God can do anything, you know—far more than you could ever imagine or guess or request in your wildest dreams! He does it not by pushing us around but by working within us, his Spirit deeply and gently within us." (Ephesians 3:20, *The Message*)

When things are falling apart around us, doesn't knowing God's power, his creative love, and his quiet working within us give us hope? How can we lay claim to the hope that is held out for us by this passage and by the many promises thoughout the Bible? We accept them by faith and live out their fulfillment. Hebrews 11:1 says, "Faith is being sure of what we hope for and certain of what we do not see." Those who are delusional may hope for the unpromised or the unrealistic—like the child who throws a penny into the fountain and wishes for a pony. But those of us who are grounded in Scripture and in the promises of God can realistically hope for whatever he has promised.

There are promises that we see fulfilled as we walk this life. God's presence is with us. He never forsakes us. He comforts us in our distress. He gives us supernatural wisdom and insights. God never makes a promise he does not fulfill—in his perfect time. And those promises give us hope even in the middle of difficult circumstances.

THURSDAY

Thoughts for today:

All of the promises God gives will be met, but their complete fulfillment will be within God's perfect timetable. In Hebrews 11, we are told that many of the heroes listed in this great faith Hall of Fame did not receive during their lifetimes the promises they had been given. They were seeing something that was yet to come. And when these heroes died, there were many promises yet to be met. Still their faith in God did not waver.

There are certain promises that are for right now and those we accept by faith and with thanksgiving. Other promises will be granted to us in God's carefully planned timing—perhaps as our lives move along and perhaps in the life to come. But we still have hope. And we are told in Romans 5:5 that "hope does not disappoint us, because God has poured out his love into our hearts by the Holy Spirit, whom he has given us."

If our hearts are full of God's love and are inhabited by the Holy Spirit, how can we live in despair? We, instead, live with hearts of rejoicing and hope in the one who has never let us down—the one who is totally and completely trustworthy. We simply have to accept in faith all that God has promised to do for us and to be to us in the present and in the future.

FRIDAY

Reading God's message

Romans 5:1–11

According to this passage, how are we justified? How is our relationship with God described as a result? What characteristics does suffering produce in our lives? What characteristic of God was he demonstrating when he sent his son to give his life for us? In Verse 11, why does the writer say we rejoice?

Journal

SATURDAY

For personal reflection

In what area of your life do you need to experience hope?

- A wayward child?
- A desperate financial situation?
- An incurable illness?
- A strangling addiction?
- A feeling of worthlessness?
- Or something else?

Whatever it is, acknowledge the situation before God in total honesty and then, in faith, commit it to him.

_____

_____

Let his peace and hope wash over you as you wait in his presence.

SUNDAY

Prayer

Father, help me to appreciate your rod of correction and your staff of guidance. They will comfort me in the dark places. Come, Lord, I will listen and obey as you lead me through the valley of my dark circumstances. You will light my steps one at a time; you assure me that I am to walk slowly and rest often. I am your loving child.

My prayer:

_____

_____

_____

_____

The Faith Life Is Filled with Hope

P r i n c i p l e   # 34

You are God's favorite child!

I had an experience once that caused my heart to ache. A woman in my Bible study and I had been talking together about prayer and about listening for God's voice. Sandy very openly responded that God had never talked to her, that feeling God's closeness didn't happen to her, and that she had never in her life had the kind of loving, communicative relationship with God that the other women in the group were talking about.

She stated that she had accepted the fact that none of the dreams she had for her life would ever come true. She knew that she just was not God's favorite child; it was as if he chose to ignore her and give his time and attention to other, more deserving, of his children. In fact, she even questioned whether she belonged in God's family at all.

I thought about those words for several days after that meeting. Finally, I realized that they haunted me so relentlessly because it was not too many years earlier that I could have said them myself. In my conversations with other Christians since then, I discovered that Sandy and I were not the only ones who ever felt that way. There are many disappointed believers who are not experiencing joy in their lives. It doesn't have to be this way.

We can live a life that connects fully to God and gives us meaning, purpose, and acceptance. Following is a recap of concepts we have studied so far. Practicing them enables our sensitivity to God to grow so that we can continue to become all that he wants us to be:

1. If God says it, I will do it.
2. Getting to the real truth about myself and about what God says will free me to be fully me.
3. I will turn toward God in total, undivided commitment and follow him every step of the way throughout my life.
4. Even when I can't understand the difficulties in my life, I will trust God because I know he is trustworthy.
5. I want to live every moment to its fullest letting God live and work through me *now*.
6. Just as I accepted God's gift of salvation by faith, I must walk the same way. Not works, just faith.

As we practice these disciplines, we will begin to realize more and more that each of us is a special and favorite child of our heavenly Father!

TUESDAY

Meditation

"God can do anything, you know—far more than you could ever imagine or guess or request in your wildest dreams! He does it not by pushing us around but by working within us, his Spirit deeply and gently within us."
(Ephesians 3:20 *The Message*)

Take time to meditate on the words of this verse and on their meaning in your life today. Allow God's gentle Spirit to speak to you. Write down thoughts that come during your meditation.

Journal

WEDNESDAY

Thoughts for today:

The principles we are choosing to follow are not complicated. More importantly, they are not dependent on our own abilities, but on God's working in us. They do not involve effort as much as they involve willingness to give up control of our lives to God. If we have the desire to have a deeply meaningful Christian life, personally connected to God, we can do it. When we commit to following God's way over our way and to walking in faith and obedience, vibrant spiritual life is within our reach.

Once we have turned our hearts and minds toward God, we are ready to look at how we can take ownership of God's great gifts and begin to experience significant growth in our faith and our spiritual lives. As we connect more meaningfully and more consistently with God, we will discover how very much we mean to him. Once we do, our lives will never be the same!

Our soul-plant will develop and be fruitful if it is exposed to the sun, given sufficient nutrients, connected to its life source, and watered regularly. We will look together at how we can expose our budding spiritual lives to these life-giving components.

THURSDAY

Thoughts for today:

Have you ever felt
- that God plays favorites and you are not one of them?
- that God sort of tolerates you, but doesn't really love you as he loves others?
- that you are on a lower rung of God's caste system?
- that talents are given to other Christians, but you have been short-changed?
- that he listens to and answers other people's prayers, but not yours?

I did feel that way a few years ago, but my life has changed since then—not because of me, but because of him. He has done the transforming, but he has assigned me a role in obedience and faithfulness, too. Our lives can be richer, fuller, happier, and more fulfilling than they presently are. They can be joyfully, and even radically, used by God.

As I listen to those who despair of a closer relationship with God, I protest the acceptance of a mediocre spiritual condition. Think of the good gifts God wants to give us! As we spend time with him, we will begin to understand how much he loves us. As we let him relate to us, our eyes are opened to his view of us and how valuable we are to him.

As we find a restful place in the lap of our heavenly Father, a change will occur in our hearts; and we will discover that each of is, in fact, God's favorite child!

FRIDAY

Reading God's message

I Corinthians 13

Read through this well known love chapter. As you do, realize that this is a perfect description of God's love for you. What characteristics of his love do you relate to most? What characteristics do you need to allow him to communicate to you better? Thank him for the extent to which he loves you.

Journal

SATURDAY

For personal reflection

What is it that you want God to do for you? What are your wildest dreams? Tell him.

_____

_____

Take your deepest desires to God in prayer and ask him to work a new life within you that will meet those desires in accordance with his perfect will. Then trust him to do it.

Make note of what you have requested and when, so you will be able to go back some time from now and verify how God met your longing—because he will do it.

_____

_____

SUNDAY

Prayer

Lord, can it really be true that you want to snuggle up close with me? You want to spend time with me? I see your face, Lord Jesus, and your eyes are filled with love and approval. It is enough.

My prayer:

_____

_____

_____

_____

_____

*Invited to
Snuggle Up Close*

P r i n c i p l e   # 35

The greatest gift we can give is our time.

God has given us a great gift in opening up the way for us to enjoy relationship with him. In return, we have to give God something precious to us before he can fulfill our deepest longings. He wants our devotion, and that devotion will be reflected in our gift of time to him. That's all. We just have to give him time. If you are following this weekly study, you are doing that. Has God honored your commitment by meeting you during these times? Are you getting to know him better? Are you beginning to feel like a dearly loved child of God?

No matter what commitments we have made in our lives and how full our schedules are, there is nothing, nothing, nothing of greater importance than giving time to God. When you sit in quietness with him, tell yourself, "This is the most important thing I have to do today." This is not self-deception. There is nothing that will fulfill our lives more than committing time to God. How do we give him time? There are a number of ways.

If we have attended church for long, we have heard people talk about daily devotions. This refers to spending time on a daily basis reading the Bible and praying so that we and God have some focused one-on-one time together. If you have never done this, today is a great day to begin. For some, this book is serving that purpose for now. On the next page are additional suggestions that may help this time be truly beneficial to your spiritual walk.

Set a goal to spend time with God every single day of the week. But it is not necessary to be *legalistic* about it. In other words, we must not feel defeated if there are days when we miss. I can guarantee, though, that once we focus daily on our relationship with God for a period of weeks and we really begin to connect with him, we will feel that we are cheating both ourselves and God if we don't take time to be with him. If we come to meet him, he will show up!

TUESDAY

Meditation

"Quiet down before God, be prayerful before him."
(Psalm 37:7a *The Message*)

Meditate on these words and ask God to make them real in your heart on a daily basis.

Journal

WEDNESDAY

Thoughts for today:

As we continue our daily walk with God we will be challenged to move beyond the perfunctory nature of a devotional routine and conduct some holy experiments.

Make your time with God truly devotional in nature—devoted to the worship of God, to learning about him, to prayer, and to hearing him respond. Of the things you are doing now during that time, assess which ones help you truly touch the heart of God and which do not. Vary your routine—take a fresh approach from time to time. No two Christians will follow exactly the same formula for this highly personalized time with God.

God talked to David while he was tending sheep, to Isaiah when he was worshipping in the temple, and to Samuel while he slept.

For me, it is important to give God the part of my day when my mind is fresh and before the hurry of the day closes in. As you begin, you may spend only a few minutes; but as you grow in comfort with this plan, it likely will expand until you find you are easily spending one-half hour to an hour in God's presence.

THURSDAY

Thoughts for today:

If you would like to rise earlier to meet with God but are having difficulty, try *asking* God to awaken you so you and he can have this time together. It may be surprising when God, rather than the alarm, does the awakening. This will tell you that God wants this time as much as you want to give it to him. He *will* wake you up! And when he does, respond by getting out of bed and getting ready to meet with him.

Whatever time of day is best for you, open this time with prayer, verbally committing the time as a sacrifice to God and asking

- that he surround you with the light of the Holy Spirit,
- that he see you through the purity of Jesus,
- that he protect you from the evil one,
- that the time you spend together will be acceptable in his sight.

You may wish to be prepared with a notebook, open to a fresh page, and dated so that if you receive any message from God, you will be ready to take notes. If there are insights you gain from the Scripture you read during this time or if God tells you something, write it down!

FRIDAY

Reading God's message

Psalm 5

As you read this psalm, observe how David spent his time with God. What time of the day is it? What are his prayer requests? What problems was David dealing with? What characteristics does he ascribe to God? How do his emotions change from the beginning to the end of the prayer?

Journal

SATURDAY

For personal reflection

You may already be having a daily personal time with God.

How can that time be made to be more worshipful?

_____

How can it become more meaningful in your walk with God?

_____

If you are not meeting God on a daily basis, commit to begin tomorrow to give him the gift of a few minutes of the day. Then do it.

God will be pleased with your gift and will honor your commitment to him by meeting you there.

SUNDAY

Prayer

Father, help me to practice being outside of time. I am tied to the clock with a ball and chain. Break that bondage, Lord God, and free me to see time as you see it—a way to keep everything from happening at once. I will wait expectantly as you break this yoke and help me to learn of you as we spend our time together. I pray in Jesus' powerful yoke-breaking name. Amen.

My prayer:

_____

_____

_____

_____

Give Him Time

P r i n c i p l e   # 36

God is not hiding. Go ahead and get to know him.

Our daily time with God is important in our spiritual lives and we begin that time with our Bible in hand and a notebook at our sides. Then we begin to talk to God asking him to honor the time that we are spending together with him. After that brief time of prayer, we can begin reading the Bible looking for what it reveals about God and his expectations of us and looking for any particular message that God may have for us that day.

In getting to know the message of the Bible, we don't have to begin at the beginning. It might be wise to start in one of the Gospels that tell the story of the life of Christ. In our reading, we will get to know Jesus' personality, we will understand how he dealt with the people around him, we will see who he accepted and who he condemned, and we will open ourselves up to what he taught. After we have read one of the Gospels, we might want to go on to some of the other New Testament books, many of which tell of the beginnings of the church, and contain the teachings of Paul, Peter, and John.

These readings will be helpful in our understanding of the historical and doctrinal foundations of our faith, but there is more to it than just collecting knowledge. The writer of Hebrews tells us this about the biblical message: "His powerful Word is sharp as a surgeon's scalpel, cutting through everything, whether doubt or defense, laying us open to listen and obey. Nothing and no one is impervious to God's Word. We can't get away from it—no matter what" (Hebrews 4:12–13 *The Message*). Our exposure to the Bible will propel our personal spiritual growth. It contains power, revelation, and insight that we will not get from any other source.

As we read our chapter or chapters for the day, we ask God to teach us through what we read. We read with the expectation that there is a message for us in the stories and in the expositions that are there. We should make note of any verses or portions of Scripture that seem to carry a special message for us at that time. Then we think on that passage, that verse, or that phrase throughout the day. God will give light to his living and powerful word as we relate to him and to others.

TUESDAY

Meditation

"Train me in good common sense; I'm thoroughly committed to living your way."
(Psalm 119:66 *The Message*)

What is God saying to you as you meditate on this text? Are you able to make this the prayer of your heart?

Journal

WEDNESDAY

Thoughts for today:

In our study of God's word, we may find that we need to read the same passage over and over again for several days before we have gleaned from it all that God wants us to have. There is no need to make a race of finishing the entire Bible. Learning its teachings is the work of a lifetime. We just need to read it consistently and with an open heart. The lessons we need to know will be revealed as we move through the text.

After reading and making notes, we move to a time of prayer. It's a good idea to experiment with physical positions that are conducive to taking our minds and hearts into the presence of God. We might spend a few minutes thinking of just one of God's attributes or one of the names by which he is called in the Bible. Or we could borrow a Scripture of worship and pray it back to God. One of my favorites is "Holy, Holy, Holy, Lord God Almighty, who is and was and is to come" (Revelation 4:8). We can enjoy learning new and creative ways to adore our God.

After we spend some time in worship of God, we continue our prayer time with thanksgiving for God's many blessings, intercession for our friends and family, confession of our sins, and requests for our own spiritual growth.

THURSDAY

Thoughts for today:

We conclude our prayer time by asking God if he has any message for us. If anything comes into our minds during that time, we should write it down assuming that it comes from God. After all, if we are in his presence, protected from Satan, saturated with God's word, and committed to him as totally as we know how to be, it is safe to assume that any thoughts at that time are given from God himself. Over time we will grow in confidence that the God of the universe (just imagine that!) is communicating with us.

As mentioned earlier, we can feel free to engage in holy experiments during this time. Ideas could include writing out our prayers, keeping a prayer request/answer list, or praying the Psalms or other passages of scripture.

Some people pray best when they are walking, others on their knees, some in the out-of-doors, some in the quiet of a holy place such as a church or a created sanctuary within the home. God is creative by nature and he loves for us to be creative in developing our relationship with him. If you have an idea, try it. If it seems to enhance our relationship with God, keep doing it. If not, try something else. The most important thing is that we are giving God the gift of time and, in doing so, we are learning to know him better.

FRIDAY

Reading God's message

Psalm 119:97–104

This psalm is the longest chapter in the Bible, containing 176 verses. In every one of those verses, the psalmist refers to God's word. He uses synonyms such as precepts, commands, law, and statutes, but they all mean messages or decrees from God. Read this passage and observe how the writer feels about God's message. How has his knowledge of God's word benefited him in his life?

Journal

SATURDAY

For personal reflection

Choose one verse from the text you are reading or from the verses that we have used for meditations each week and commit it to memory.

Write it on a 3" x 5" card and carry it with you until you know it well.

Then ponder those words; let God speak to you through the Scripture you have taken into your heart.

Move on to memorize other verses so that they are available for God to call to your memory when he wants to speak to you.

SUNDAY

Prayer

Fill my heart with the passion of finding you, Lord. Keep my heart whole and undivided. Purify my motives; I want to be like you, Jesus. The desire to be one with you and the Father is planted in me; strengthen this plant so it can be an oak of righteousness, rooted and grounded so nothing can blow it over.

My prayer:

_____

_____

_____

_____

_____

Conversation of the Heart

Principle # 37

No personal sacrifice that we make for God will go unrewarded.

When we first fell in love, we were totally committed to our lover. We never tired of sitting in his/her presence, of just being together, of breathing the same air. There might be times when we have a similar longing to grow closer to God and, in an effort to do so, we offer to give him a longer period than our daily devotional time. Jesus himself is our example here. We find a number of references in the Gospel accounts of his earthly life indicating that he went off by himself for time alone with his heavenly Father. He sometimes spent all night in prayer and communion with God. If Jesus felt the longing to give the gift of lengthy, devoted time to his Father, how can we do less?

Sometimes when we have time at home alone, we can give God the sacrifice of an afternoon or an evening devoted to learning of him, to prayer, to meditation, to song, to fasting, and to reading his word. If alone time at home is impossible, we may need to go somewhere away from home. My spiritual friend and I have gone off for overnight times on several occasions just to allow God to wash over us in uninterrupted time. I know that when I choose to do this, I cannot *demand* that God come in and do something great for me, but I have found that every time I have given him these extended periods of time, he has visited my spirit, communed with me, and has drawn me closer to himself. He often uses this focused time that I offer in order to give some direction or confirmation of direction in my life.

These are also times when we can enter, once again, into some holy experiments, including meditation. We have been working on some meditation each week, but we might be able to take the practice to new levels as we mature spiritually. The goal of meditation is to take our eyes off of things on earth and turn them without distraction to God. The only way to do that is to quiet the competing voices in our heads. You know what I mean: the negative self-talk, the to-do list that keeps nagging at us, the doubts that God is really listening when we pray, and the regrets over past failures. Meditation tunes out those voices and tunes in God's. Whose voice would we rather hear?

T U E S D A Y

M e d i t a t i o n

**"I meditate on your name all night, God,
treasuring your revelation, O God."**
(Psalm 119:55 *The Message*)

Ponder the message of this verse allowing God's word to penetrate your heart and conform you to what he would have you to be.

J o u r n a l

W E D N E S D A Y

T h o u g h t s   f o r   t o d a y :

If we are ready to take our relationship with God to a new level, we might look seriously at God's invitation to meditate on him and his word. Here's one way to practice meditation. Sit in a chair with a straight back. Sit up straight, but comfortable with your feet flat on the floor. Your hands should be resting naturally in your lap. Now practice a couple of relaxation techniques: Focus on the muscles in your toes, your feet, your ankles, up each leg, your thighs, your hips, your torso, your fingers, your arms, your shoulders, your neck, your face. Tense the muscles one by one, then relax them.

Then focus on your breathing. Fill your lungs as fully as possible, hold your breath for several seconds, then exhale slowly through your nose. When you exhale, get rid of all the air in your lungs. Do this several times until your body feels oxygenated and you are relaxed. Your mind is not thinking about anything, you are paying attention to your breath. Pause. Take yourself to the presence of God and listen. Don't think. Just listen. Take as much time as you need.

If it helps to keep the thoughts at bay, repeat a word over and over again so that your mind is, as much as possible, emptied of your own thoughts. Stay relaxed, focus on breathing, focus on one word—then listen. When he speaks, you will know.

THURSDAY

Thoughts for today:

Another way to detach from our earthly desires and focus our attention solely on God is to practice the spiritual discipline of fasting. We should never use fasting as a way to twist God's arm or to make him feel obligated to answer our prayers. Instead, we are simply willing to give up something we like as a sacrifice so that God alone is the focus of our attention. There is something about experiencing hunger that reminds us that we are doing this in honor of and for the love of God and that we do it gladly as a token gift of commitment to him. It is at the end of times of fasting that we often get our clearest messages from God.

We may choose to fast for periods of time from sweets, television, secular music, or some other enjoyment that we are willing to give up as a sacrifice to God. When we experience a craving for that which we have given up, we will be reminded of our devotion to God and God alone. We do not want our commitment to him to be hindered by anything here on earth.

If we practice these spiritual disciplines, we will know that the meditation was worth the time we gave it, and the fasting was worth whatever discomfort we may have felt. Best of all, we will sense the pleasure of God at our commitment to knowing him.

FRIDAY

Reading God's message

Matthew 6:5–18

Read the instructions Jesus gives in this passage for prayer and for fasting. Where should you pray? What should you not do when you pray? What do we learn about dependence upon God from the prayer that Jesus taught? What role does forgiveness play in effective prayer? Who is the audience for our fasting? Does Jesus seem to expect that we will fast? Are you willing to be obedient to his expectation?

Journal

SATURDAY

For   personal   reflection

What gift can you give to God this week?

_____

Should you give him the gift of a larger than normal period of time?

_____

Should you give up something so you can focus more completely on him?

_____

Should you practice meditation?

_____

Ask God what gift he would like and then give it to him just as soon as you can. He will honor your commitment to make him of first importance in your life.

SUNDAY

Prayer

You gave me the gift of yourself, dear Jesus. Now, I want to give you my time and my life. There is no sacrifice that I make on earth that is comparable to the great sacrifice you made for me. I give you all of me, Lord, and ask that you continue to reveal yourself to me so that we can know each other better. Amen.

My prayer:

_____

_____

_____

_____

Give Him Greater Gifts Sometime

P r i n c i p l e   # 38

Find a teacher and learn all you can.
Then find a student and teach all you know.

When God brought us into his spiritual family, we joined with other brothers and sisters who are at varying stages of intimacy with our Father. We all fit just perfectly into that family and, just as our earthly families work and play together and teach one another, the same pattern is true in our spiritual family. We will be able to give great boosts to our spiritual growth if we learn to benefit from the insights, methods, and nuggets of wisdom already discovered by other Christians. Both joy and strength come from our journeying together.

It is important that we find a church in which we can participate and grow. When we get together with our fellow churchgoers on Sunday, we have the opportunity *to listen to scriptural preaching.* The pastors of our churches may or may not be world-class preachers, but we need to learn all that we can as we listen with open hearts and open Bibles.

Another benefit that we gain from meeting together is joy of *worshipping as a body of God followers.* It is so important that we, as believers, gather together to worship God corporately. The problem with that plan is that worship is an emotional experience and we will all admit that we don't always feel like getting revved up into a meaningful worship experience just because it is scheduled on a Sunday morning.

Here are a couple suggestions that might make that experience more meaningful for us: First, we should prepare ahead of time by spending time in personal worship and/or prayer before heading out to the church service. That way we will have already entered God's presence and won't feel that the emotional involvement when we get to the church is in any way contrived or driven by some kind of manipulation on the part of the worship leader or team. Our participation at that point is more likely to be a genuine act of worship. If we get to church and still don't feel like entering in emotionally, we should just pray and tell God that we are offering to him a sacrifice of praise. Then we simply offer as a gift of love to God our involvement in the corporate worship experience. God will accept this as a sacrifice of our personal and selfish desires on the altar of worship to him. I think he likes that. And before we know it, we will, too!

TUESDAY

Meditation

"Run after mature righteousness—faith, love, peace—joining those who are in honest and serious prayer before God."
(II Timothy 2:22b *The Message*)

Think about what this verse teaches about what our goals should be and about the kind of people who can help us reach those goals. Allow the Holy Spirit to make this message alive to you.

Journal

WEDNESDAY

Thoughts for today:

It is vitally important that we not only engage in devotional Bible reading but also that we dig in and study to know in a greater depth the meaning of God's word and its message to us. That study can often best be accomplished in a group. The group commits to a certain study, to spending time on homework outside of the sessions, and then to meeting together to discuss what has been learned. I recommend that you make every effort to be involved in a small group Bible study.

Most churches offer them, but we may have to ask questions in order to find a group that is specifically suited to each of us. The friendships that develop in these groups will be long-lasting; and the support we are able to offer one another in terms of prayer, concern, and accountability will be immeasurable.

There are times when there is no Bible study or worship service scheduled, but we still want to learn from others. One way to do that is to read good books. Sometimes an effective author can communicate an insight or thought in a way that touches us on an intellectual or emotional level and thus enlightens our thinking or challenges us to a greater level of commitment to God. Find your favorite Christian authors and then keep good books readily available to fill your mind with transforming thoughts.

THURSDAY

Thoughts for today:

We can add to our learning by listening to preaching tapes available through Christian publishers or Christian radio. So much is available to us these days that we have no excuses for not exposing ourselves to good Bible teaching. Through these various means, we can hear preaching on current topics that will engage us in spiritual disciplines, encourage our growth toward God, help us to understand application of Christian teaching to the world around us, and fill our minds with knowledge of God's word.

An important way that we can strengthen one another spiritually is by entering into a mentoring relationship with someone who can teach us and encourage us to grow in our relationships to God and to others. Once growth begins, it may be time to seek another mentoring relationship with someone whom we can *teach*. Remember that Jesus sent his disciples out two-by-two. I believe this was so they could provide guidance, support, and accountability to each other. His plan is still effective for spiritual vitality today. One-on-one discipleship encourages growth both in the one who teaches and in the one who is taught.

We don't have to know everything all at once, but we grow exponentially when we find ways to learn as much as possible from those who know more than we do about theology and the ways to live a vital Christian life.

FRIDAY

Reading God's message

I Corinthians 12:12–31

This passage describes Christians as being part of a body. How does Paul say the body parts are to treat one another? Who decides what part you play in the body? Why did God give various gifts or abilities to members of the body? How does the unity of purpose required for a body to function help us understand how we help one another mature in our relationship to God?

Journal

SATURDAY

For   personal   reflection

Think of mature Christians in your life. Who can you learn from? What can you learn? No matter where you are in your spiritual walk, you can find someone who is farther down the path and can encourage you along the way.

Pray for God's leading. Then schedule a lunch or coffee with that person and ask them to talk to you about their faith.

If you sense an openness and a leading of God, ask this person if he or she will mentor you in your Christian life.

At the very least, ask this person for advice that you can put into practice as you grow in your relationship with God.

Then ask God to lead you to someone who is struggling in their walk with God.

Offer to meet with him/her and teach them what God has been teaching you.

SUNDAY

Prayer

Holy Spirit, you are the teacher and you dwell within me. Give me the grace to sit quietly and absorb your word. You have given me a taste and I want more. I can feel my soul growing stronger and my spirit muscles expanding. Lord, it's so great to be fit for you! Help me to find someone who will exercise with me; you enjoy watching your children grow strong in you together.

My prayer:

_____

_____

_____

_____

Learn From Others

P r i n c i p l e   # 39

The gifts of devotion we give to God open the passageway to heaven so that his love can freely flow back to us.

We studied earlier about Brother Lawrence, a layperson of the seventeenth century, working in a monastery kitchen just outside of Paris. All the while he worked at preparing meals, serving the monks, and washing pots and pans, he talked with God. He was not even a real monk, he was just a layman—sort of a second class citizen in the monk department, but he valued his relationship with God more than he valued anything else in this world.

Brother Lawrence determined that he would spend his time in constant communication with God. After all, he reasoned, if God was present with him, it would be nothing less than rudeness to ignore him. So Lawrence determined to drive "away from my mind everything that was capable of interrupting my thought of God" (Spire Books, 1967, p.2). As he approached the end of his life, he confessed that it had taken nearly ten years of focused concentration before the continual communication with God became habitual. But, by the time he died at over eighty years of age, he had spent more than thirty years in unbroken conversation with his heavenly Father.

The more years he lived in constant communication with God, the more evident it became that he and God had developed a special relationship. One contemporary described Brother Lawrence as one who was caressed by God. Recognizing his access to God's wisdom, people began to write to him for advice. Others came from miles around to be spiritually taught by him and by his example. He has inspired many to keep God constantly at the forefront of their thoughts and in continuous communication.

If we want to practice this continual conversation with God, we may need reminders of God's presence in our lives. Maybe just looking at the clock becomes our reminder to pray. We might write verses of Scripture on cards and put them on our mirrors, next to our telephones, in our middle desk drawers, or on our refrigerators so they can serve as God-reminders throughout our days.

When we are so reminded, we should pray, briefly turning our minds and thoughts toward heaven. The more we acknowledge God's presence in our lives by communicating with him, the more our friendship with God will grow. It is a matter of choice. Do we want to focus on things of this world or on our relationship with God? The rewards of the choosing a God focus are great. You and I can experience the caresses of God just as Brother Lawrence did!

TUESDAY

Meditation

"Don't fret or worry. Instead of worrying, pray. Let petitions and praises shape your worries into prayers, letting God know your concerns. Before you know it, a sense of God's wholeness, everything coming together for good, will come and settle you down. It's wonderful what happens when Christ displaces worry at the center of your life."
(Philippians 4:6–7 *The Message*)

Meditate on the instructions given in these verses and then on the concept of Christ replacing worry in your life.

Journal

WEDNESDAY

Thoughts for today:

As growing Christians we engage in spiritual activities not because we expect any great gifts to be returned from God. We study, worship, and pray because it is a joy to give something back to God in return for all he has done for us. Everything we learn from God's word tells us that we don't "pay in" the right behavior so that God will treat us better, love us more, or do good things for us. God loves us no matter how we behave and he has already done for us more than we could ever deserve. We give these gifts of devotion to God out of hearts of love, out of our desire to live a more spiritually connected meaningful life, and out of faith in the God who said he would reward those who seek him.

When we do seek God and show our sincerity of heart by our activities and attitudes, we begin to feel his love. We always knew that it was there, but now it begins to become more real. We may have had all kinds of blockages within us that kept us from receiving God's love. But as we seek him, the love receptors in our hearts develop and become unblocked, and we begin to feel the love that he has been sending to us all along and we begin to experience what it feels like to be God's child.

THURSDAY

Thoughts for today:

As we get to know God better, we begin to discover that our time with him gives him a chance to reveal himself to us. This time with him positions us in God's presence so that we can delight in his grace and love.

We will begin to look forward to these times of communion with him. He is never harsh with us. He is always loving, always caring, always looking out for what is best for us. Why wouldn't we want to be in the presence of someone who cares so much for us?

Psalm 34:8 (*The Message*) says, "Open your mouth and taste, open your eyes and see—how good God is." Once we taste, we will find that the taste is sweet and we will want more, and more. He who sees these blossoming, secret, devotional lives of ours will reward us. After time, people around us will begin to notice a peace we did not have before. They will notice that we are relating to others with more love than we used to have. They will notice that we have a quietness and depth that they never saw in us before. They will see our purposeful, meaningful lives and wonder what our secret to success could be. But the greatest thing of all is that we will begin loving being loved by God, and we will find ourselves knowing that we are among his favorite children!

FRIDAY

Reading God's message

Romans 8:28–39

What reassurances of God's love do you find in this passage? List them. Is this teaching real to your heart or just an intellectual assent? As you get to know God better, you will find you can trust him to love you completely.

Journal

SATURDAY

For personal reflection

Today, practice
- turning your worries into prayers,
- expressing to God your feelings and your needs,
- talking to God about what you are involved in,
- letting him know what your dreams are, and
- allowing him to shape them.

Also, spend some time in prayer today thanking God for
- the gift of relationship with him,
- forgiveness of sin,
- the joy of human relationships, and
- the abundance of provisions he has given you.

Expand this thanksgiving list so that you can see more clearly how fully God has expressed his love for you. Receive God's love and enjoy the relationship that he has offered.

SUNDAY

Prayer

Jesus, be my first love in truth. Let it not be just words that sound good. You are the only one with whom I will spend the rest of my life—no other love comes with that kind of guarantee. You can never be lost from me. You are the living, resurrected Jesus now and forevermore. Amen.

My prayer:

_____

_____

_____

_____

You Can't Outgive God

Cultivating a Worshipping Heart

P r i n c i p l e   # 40

Our lives must be about God alone, not God and ....

What image comes to our minds when we think of the term "worship"? We might see Arab followers of Islam dropping to their knees on their prayer rugs five times a day. That is devotion, but is it worship? We might think of Christians gathered on a Sunday morning singing hymns of praise. That is a church service, but is it worship? It is our tendency to think of worship in terms of form or liturgy, when, in reality, true worship is an action that grows spontaneously out of an attitude that we consciously cultivate within our very being.

That attitude of worship is a natural response to the kind of life of God-connection to which we aspire. Before we can be worshippers, we must be committed followers, and when we adopt the life of following God and his word, worship will be spontaneous. Given such a prepared heart, what a joy and privilege it is to engage in worship! We don't need a muezzin to call from a minaret to remind us to get down on our knees, we don't need an 11:00 o'clock Sunday morning service to get us in the mood for God; instead, worship flows out of our very lives and out of the depths of our souls. And the worship is directed solely to the God whom we are growing to love and adore.

In the Webster definition of worship, the words reverence, honor, homage, regard, and adoration are used in various contexts.

- What is it that we reverence in our lives?
- What do we honor?
- To what do we pay homage?
- What or whom do we hold in high regard?
- What or whom do we adore?

These are matters of the heart, and they require our truthful introspection under the guidance of the Holy Spirit. Of course, as committed Christians we want to think that God is the one we revere, honor, regard, adore, and pay homage to. And he deserves to be. But before we can offer him devoted worship, we have to make sure that there is no other person, job, activity, approval, or goal getting the worship that should be going to God alone. In other words, in order to worship the God of the universe, we have to get rid of the lesser gods that may be holding a place in our hearts. That's where we begin in cultivating a heart of worship.

TUESDAY

Meditation

Think about the words in the following verses and ponder them as God opens his heart to yours. Meditate on what this passage tells you about your active involvement in your own spiritual maturity.

"We use our powerful God-tools for smashing warped philosophies, tearing down barriers erected against the truth of God, fitting every loose thought and emotion and impulse into the structure of life shaped by Christ. Our tools are ready at hand for clearing the ground of every obstruction and building lives of obedience into maturity."
(II Corinthians 10:5–6 *The Message*)

Journal

WEDNESDAY

Thoughts for today:

In her book, *How to Live Right When Your Life Goes Wrong*, psychologist Leslie Vernick helps us sort out the lesser gods (she refers to them as idols) that may be priorities for us:
"How do we know if we have idols in our heart? Take them away and watch your reaction. What happens to you when you don't have power and control? When you don't have peace and serenity? When you don't have pleasure or approval? When you don't have respect or security? When you don't have a fat bank account? When you are not recognized for your accomplishments? When you are ignored or humiliated? What happens to you when you don't get your way? We often don't know our heart is so attached to our idols until they're threatened. Then we fight like mad to keep them!"
(Waterbrook Press, 2003, p. 94).

Do we recognize any of our own idols in that list? We are creatures who are created to worship, but that natural bent to worship has been distorted by sin and by our now fallen natures. Therefore, while it was God's original design to have us naturally and completely worship him, Satan's temptation entered in and that design has been skewed.

We still have the desire and inclination to worship, but our tendency has become to worship the wrong gods. Until we recognize this and give up those lesser gods, we will not be able to worship God in a way that is unobstructed, undiluted, and undivided.

THURSDAY

Thoughts for today:

There may be lesser gods in our lives that are blocking our relationship with God. Once we have rid ourselves of those obstructions, we are prepared to receive God's love and worship him in the fullness of our spirits. We begin by asking the Holy Spirit to enlighten us concerning the things to which we give more emotional loyalty than we do to God.

Let's agree that there is nothing, not any thing that is so desirable to us that it is worth sacrificing our relationship with God. Then, we can tell him that we recognize that our desire for prestige, financial security, approval of others, control, being right, pleasure, love of another human—we will name whatever it is—has become a god to us and that we are willing to give it up in our devotion to him and in our desire to love and worship him alone. He will accept the sacrifice that we make. He will understand the emotional pain it causes us to do so. He will honor the honesty of our hearts, will comfort us, and draw us close.

Perhaps for the first time in our lives, there is nothing to block the infinite, perfect, and compelling love that God wants to give us. We can now receive it in its fullness. And when we do, the natural and almost uncontrollable response will be worship.

FRIDAY

Reading God's message

II Corinthians 6:14–7:1

What kinds of separateness from the world and sin is Paul writing about in these verses? What rationale does he give for living such separated lives? What promise does God give for those who are willing to separate from sin? What is our motivation (7:1) for living holy and pure lives?

Journal

SATURDAY

F o r   p e r s o n a l   r e f l e c t i o n

It is very important in your spiritual development that you inspect your heart, your mind, and your life and discover anything there (you may find a number of things) that comes between you and God.

What is there that has more control over you than God does?

_____

What is there that you are not willing to give up even if God were to ask you to do so?

_____

Identify the idols in your life. Is there anything in those idols that is worth hanging on to if it means giving up a wholehearted commitment to God?

_____

Give everything up to God and ask for his power to overcome the encroachment of idols that come between you and him.

SUNDAY

P r a y e r

Lord, let's have a garage sale of all the junk in my heart and mind. Would you help me sort it out, Holy Spirit, so I know what to throw out and what to keep? I will agree with you and ruthlessly clean house. I want an uncluttered, clean, holy tabernacle for you. With more room, you can fill me more with your love, joy, and peace. That is your desire for me, too. We are in agreement. Hallelujah!

My prayer:

_____

_____

_____

_____

Cultivating a Worshipping Heart

P r i n c i p l e   # 41

Adoration is an outward expression of our inward devotion to God.

As II Corinthians 7:1 (*The Message*) tells us, once we have cleansed our lives of all that defiles us, we are "fit and holy temples for the worship of God." Once we have rid ourselves of the idols that distract us from meaningful connection with God, our unencumbered hearts begin to receive the love God so lavishly gives, and we find that we are ready and eager to worship.

How do we worship God in a way that is consistent with what Scripture tells us about what our worship should consist of? What do we do when we come before God in worship? There are a number of worship-filled actions we can take, but one very important way is simply to express our adoration for God.

We use the word *adore* in our culture today in a way that is somewhat different from how it was used in its original derivation. Today we say we adore babies and puppies. We adore a certain color or a particular flower. We adore being adored. The original word, however, came from the Latin verb *orare*, which means "to speak." From it we get such words as *orator* (speaker), *oracle* (prophesy), and *oratorio* (musical prayer). The word *orison*, a derivation from the same Latin word but which is no longer used, actually means *to pray* or *adore*.

The word's history carries the idea not only of veneration, of respect, and of attraction, but also the idea of expressing those emotions *out loud* in words that we would call prayers of adoration. Just *feeling* adoration is not enough. Expression of it in words is part and parcel of the very concept of adoration. And adoration is an essential part of true worship.

God deserves sincere adoration. We worship him just because of who he is, not because of something he has done for us, not because he has answered our prayers. Just because he is God, he deserves to be adored. When we approach God in worship we should tell him just that. We want to tell him that we love him, that we honor him for being the creator and sustainer of the universe, that we submit to his will for us because he is God, and that we bow in reverence before him. The more we worship, the more we become comfortable in God's presence and the more we sense his receptivity to our adoration. Our relationship with God becomes stronger, and we feel a tug to worship to greater degrees.

TUESDAY

Meditation

So here's what I want you to do, God helping you: Take your everyday, ordinary life—your sleeping, eating, going-to-work, and walking-around life—and place it before God as an offering."
(Romans 12:1a *The Message*)

Ponder the meaning of these words. Then think about your everyday life and visualize giving each portion of your daily routine over to God as an offering to him.

Journal

WEDNESDAY

Thoughts   for   today:

Sometimes it may be hard to know what to say as we offer adoration to God. One thing that is helpful is to look for passages of worship in the Bible. If such an expression is written in the Bible, it must be, in God's eyes, an acceptable form of worship. So we can choose one of those prayers, chants, or hymns from a biblical passage and use it in a given time of worship as we prayerfully repeat the words to God.

On another day, we may choose a different passage to offer him. Other times, our own words of worship just flow and we may not need to use a Scriptural passage. Here are a few selections of prayers of adoration and worship taken from the book of Revelation. We will find others as we search Scriptures.

Revelation 4:8 Holy, holy, holy is the Lord God Almighty, who was, and is, and is to come.

Revelation 5:12–13 Worthy is the Lamb…to receive power and wealth and wisdom and strength and honor and glory and praise!

Revelation 11:17–18 We give thanks to you, Lord God Almighty, the One who is and who was, because you have taken your great power and have begun to reign.

Revelation 15:3–4 Great and marvelous are your deeds, Lord God Almighty. Just and true are your ways, King of the ages…you alone are holy…. .

THURSDAY

Thoughts for today:

When we peer into heaven through John's writing in the book of Revelation, we come to the conclusion that we will spend a great deal of eternity simply worshipping and adoring God. If that is the case, this world is our practice room for making our worship acceptable to God. We should make it our goal to have worship in heaven be a simple extension of what we have already practiced on earth.

We would be well advised not only to look for ways to worship God and to find words with which to worship him, but also to seek reasons to offer him our adoration. "Hallelujah! For our Lord God Almighty reigns. Let us rejoice and be glad and give him glory!" (Revelation 19:6–7). Why is the great multitude in Revelation worshipping God? Because He reigns. That's all. That's reason enough to be happy and give him honor. What reasons can we think of to worship God? His righteousness? His power? His goodness? His mercy? His creation? His holiness?

We need to realize and embrace the concept that if God never did anything for us, he is worthy of adoration and worship just because he is God. The more we tell him this, the more he will reveal himself and his character to us and the more natural it will be for us to honor and revere him.

FRIDAY

Reading God's message

Isaiah 12

Read this passage of worship. Why is the writer praising God? What has God provided for his people? What feelings does Isaiah write about now that God has responded? What does he want the nations to know about the God of Israel? Who does he want to join him in this song of worship?

Journal

SATURDAY

For personal reflection

Practice adoring God.

For today, and maybe a few more, don't ask God for anything when you pray. Instead, simply bow in adoration before him and let him know that if he never does anything more for you, you will

- love him,
- worship him, and
- adore him.

He is God and worthy of your love. Tell him so.

SUNDAY

Prayer

Enlighten me, Holy Spirit, to know what adoring you looks like. Develop me in this area of my life. Bring me to wholeness in knowing how to worship you. Somehow I sense it has to do with how I feel about me. Unlock the door of the room that is housing this secret. Give me faith to peek inside without fear. In your powerful name I ask. Amen.

My prayer:

_____

_____

_____

_____

Offer Your Adoration

P r i n c i p l e # 42

Worship that doesn't move us probably won't move God either!

One way we can express our worship to God is through music. God's word is full of directives to bring our musical offerings to him. Here's an example from Psalm 150:3–6:

- Praise him with the sounding of the trumpet,
- Praise him with the harp and lyre,
- Praise him with tambourine and dancing,
- Praise him with the strings and flute,
- Praise him with the clash of cymbals,
- Praise him with resounding cymbals.
- Let everything that has breath praise the Lord. Praise the Lord.

Just listen to the cadence the psalmist describes, the variety of expressions of praise! It sounds as if its writer understood how to praise God with an enthusiastic gift of music from his very heart.

In Paul's letters to the New Testament church, he also instructs Christians to sing hymns and spiritual songs and to make music in their hearts to God. It is apparent that God likes to hear us express our worship to him through music. Some of us are more musically inclined than others, but whatever our musical talent may be, it is a gift God has given us, and he delights when we give it back to him.

For me it is a joy to read some of the words to old hymns. I love to find a classic hymnal and read the true worship poetry that these saints of old have written. If we memorize some of the stanzas that are most meaningful to us, we can offer the words and music as praise to God as we go through our days.

If we immerse ourselves in good Christian music, we can hum along and even sing along when we feel like it—as loudly as we want to when we're home alone or in the car by ourselves. It may not sound good to us, but we can be sure that it is beautiful music to the holy ears of God. Let's not relegate music in worship only to Sunday mornings or praise gatherings with other believers.

Let's keep singing our praises to God. Musical worship can run through our minds and out our mouths as we iron clothes, drive to work, or work out at the gym. These musical offerings direct our thoughts, attention, and hearts toward God all day long. He enjoys and appreciates such worship. God wants us to use music as a tool to praise him and to stir our emotions in praise even when the entire attendance at a worship service is just you or me and God. He is a highly receptive audience!

TUESDAY

Meditation

"Sing songs from your heart to Christ. Sing praises over everything, any excuse for a song to God the Father in the name of our master, Jesus Christ."
(Ephesians 5:19–20 *The Message*)

Meditate on these words. Focus on singing from your heart. Focus on praising God over everything. Ask God to show you something you should praise him for right now.

Journal

WEDNESDAY

Thoughts for today:

Another way we can worship God is by using our bodies as instruments of praise. If you have ever watched movies set in old England or read old English novels, you have probably come across the English wedding vow that says, "With my body, I thee worship." Can you imagine someone saying that to you? It is a great vow of total commitment, loyalty, and devoted love.

In our relationship with God, he expects nothing less than commitment of body, mind, soul, and spirit. Romans 12:1 says, "...offer your bodies as living sacrifices, holy and pleasing to God—this is your spiritual act of worship."

If our bodies are important in our worship, it is important that we take good care of them. Exercise helps to keep us agile so that we can bow before God or so we can kneel even for extended periods of time. Keeping ourselves limber and in shape allows us to sit in meditation without our muscles forcing the time of meditation to premature conclusion.

David used his body in worshipful expression by dancing before the Lord; but in order to dance, we have to be in the kind of physical shape that allows dancing. Our workouts and walks can be acts of worship as we learn to care for the body God has given us.

THURSDAY

Thoughts for today:

We worship God with our bodies knowing that on this earth, our bodies will be full of imperfection. God only asks that we offer back to him what he has given to us. We should eat healthily, exercise when we can, and honor God with our bodies in whatever condition they are in. God will accept the best kind of worship we can offer. Just as we talked about conducting holy experiments in our quiet time with God, so we can experiment with different kinds of worship with our bodies if we are in the physical condition to do so.

The Bible often speaks of kneeling or bowing before God. Psalm 95:6, says "Come, let us bow down in worship, let us kneel before the Lord our Maker." Our physical bowing before God shows our reverence for him, our acknowledgment that he is almighty and to be honored as we would honor an earthly king. Scripture tells us that every knee will bow before him when he appears. Why would he not deserve our bowing now even though we do not see him physically?

Others find that raising hands toward heaven in a symbolic connection with God enhances their worship experience. Let's offer him our bodies—including our knees, our arms, and our voices—in worship and see what he does with our offering. After all, Jesus gave his body for us. Why would we do less for him?

FRIDAY

Reading God's message

Psalm 68:24–35

Read this psalm observing the ways in which the people of Israel worshipped God. How does the psalmist describe God? What phrases define the praises and thanksgiving of the people?

Journal

SATURDAY

For personal reflection

In what way do you need to let your guard down more as you begin to worship meaningfully from your heart?

Do you need to be open to moving more freely? Experiment with that in your alone times with God.

Do you need to allow the music of your soul to overflow in heartfelt praise to God?

Don't be afraid to sing out loud. God accepts the spirit of the gift, not its musical quality.

Commit today to giving God your enthusiasm in worship with your song and your body.

SUNDAY

Prayer

I need to tell you, Father, that worship has been a foreign word to me. I need help in quieting my brain to let my heart go free to express itself to you. There is still shame in being free to worship you openly. Deliver me, Lord. You tell me in your word that you are the great deliverer. I will keep my eyes on you while you set me free. In your holy name, Jesus, I pray. Amen.

My prayer:

_____

_____

_____

_____

Sing and Dance Your Worship

P r i n c i p l e   # 43

Love, by its very nature, must give gifts!

Many artists have depicted the visit of the wise men to baby Jesus and have entitled their paintings, "The Adoration of the Magi." We agree that adoration is a part of worship. But we also find that when the magi came to adore the Christ-child, they did not come empty-handed. They brought gifts. Sacrificial, extravagant gifts were evidence of their devotion. Giving gifts to our creator will flow naturally out of hearts of true worship.

We worship God in giving gifts of money, time, and talents. As we give the gifts, we realize and acknowledge that we have no resources, talents, health, or blessings that have not come from the loving hand of God, and what we are doing is merely giving back to him out of what he has already given to us.

Giving is a part of worship and one that we should practice to the fullest extent possible—with cheerfulness. The more we give, the more our heartfelt gifts will become a natural part of our worship experience. We need to think creatively about what we can give. Gifts of money come immediately to mind and should be given freely. There is much scriptural teaching on giving of money which instructs us, first of all, to give regularly. Paul tells the churches to bring offerings of money to God "on the first day of the week." In other words, we must not wait until we have plenty or until our proverbial ship comes in. We must give to God and his work consistently.

Then we are told to give sacrificially, whether it is the gift of ourselves, our time, or our money. Even if we have to give up something for ourselves in order to do so, we are told to give. Even if the gift we offer is small, we are told to give. The sincerity of our worship is measured by our hearts, not by the amount of our gift.

II Corinthians 9:7 (*The Message*) tells us, "God loves it when the giver delights in the giving." If we have a tendency to hang on to everything we have, we need to be careful how committed to God we become because our very commitment may cause us to give away more than we intended to! But we will be happy in doing it, and we know that God will honor and reward a heart filled with gifts of generous and overflowing worship. So let's give freely.

TUESDAY

Meditation

**"Bring gifts and celebrate,
Bow down before the beauty of God,
Then to your knees—everyone worship!"**
(Psalm 96:8b–9 *The Message*)

Meditate on these words and ask God to reveal to you the significance of bringing gifts as an act of worship. What creative gifts is he asking you to give? Enjoy a time of meditation and worship.

Journal

WEDNESDAY

Thoughts for today:

In Luke 21, we are told of one day when Jesus sat watching people walk by the treasury in the temple at Jerusalem, dropping into it their offerings. He pointed out to those around him the poverty-stricken widow who put in an offering equivalent to a couple of pennies. He said that she had given more than all the others he had observed because "she out of her poverty put in all she had to live on" (Luke 21:4b). Jesus seemed more interested in what the giver had left over than in the amount of money dropped into the treasury.

Paul, in II Corinthians 8:2–3 (*The Message*), tells of people in churches of a particular area who were experiencing many problems. He says, "They were incredibly happy, though desperately poor. The pressure triggered something totally unexpected: an outpouring of pure and generous gifts…They gave offerings of whatever they could—far more than they could afford!"

Paul goes on to explain, in Verse 5, another important insight about the giving of our resources, "They had first given themselves unreservedly to God and to us. The other giving simply flowed out of the purposes of God working in their lives." In other words, if we give our devotion to God first, the giving will naturally follow.

THURSDAY

Thoughts for today:

Of course, we know that we need to give financial gifts to God. But there are many other ways we can sacrificially and worshipfully give meaningful gifts to God, as well. Here are a few ideas:

- Offer God a Sunday afternoon where just you and he take a walk together.
- Offer God your time and the use of your car to take an elderly neighbor shopping or to medical appointments.
- Offer him the use of your living room to host a neighborhood Bible study.
- Offer him your lunch hour to spend time with a coworker struggling in a difficult marriage.
- Offer him a share of the bounty of your garden by giving it to the local soup kitchen.

We will be able to think of other gifts that come specifically from our resources, our talents, and our hearts. Where is there a need that we can fill? Who in our lives needs a special touch? What needs to be done at our churches? Or in our neighborhoods? Where do gifts that we can give fit best into the kingdom of God?

The concept of holy experiments can apply as we consider all that we can give to our God, our maker. It is the attitude that matters most to him. What are we willing to sacrifice for God? What are we willing to go without?

FRIDAY

Reading God's message

II Corinthians 8:1–15 and 9:6–12

Read these passages on giving gifts. List all of the characteristics of a giver who pleases God.

Journal

SATURDAY

For personal reflection

What can you give to God today? This week?

_____

_____

Begin to adopt an attitude of giving in place of an attitude of getting. What can you do or give that would bring pleasure to your heavenly Father?

_____

_____

Ask God what he would like you to give. Then do it with cheerfulness. He will respond with love and his love will bring you joy!

SUNDAY

Prayer

Lord, as you know, I am grateful for the gifts of good things that you have given me. Help me, now, to take my eyes off the gifts and place them onto you, the giver. When I do that, I want to offer back to you all that you have given to me. Show me how to do that in ways that honor your holy name, in which I pray. Amen.

My prayer:

_____

_____

_____

_____

Give God Worshipful Gifts

P r i n c i p l e   # 44

Worship shared is worship magnified.

Praise is an expression of gratitude and devotion to God in return for all that he has done for us. Praise is the part of worship where we get to say thank you to God for his great blessings, for his answered prayers, for his power working in our lives, for his unconditional love, and for his gifts, which are poured out moment by moment.

In his book, *Reflections on the Psalms*, C. S. Lewis confesses that at one time in his Christian life he had a problem with the idea of a God who demanded praise. Such a demand seemed, from his human perspective, as egotistical. Surely if any of us demanded praise from other humans, we would be looked upon with suspicion. Ultimately, however, Lewis came to the realization that when we love or enjoy something or someone, that delight is not complete until we express it. If you are in love, you are restless and unfulfilled until you are free enough to express that love to the person whom you adore. The same is true in our relationship to God; therefore, God wants us to praise him as a means of fulfillment of the joy we feel in our relationship with him. As Lewis concludes, "We delight to praise what we enjoy because the praise not merely expresses but completes the enjoyment…Fully to enjoy is to glorify. In commanding us to glorify Him, God is inviting us to enjoy Him" (Collins Clear-Type Press, 1961, p.81).

Enjoying God will include praising him just as surely as being in love includes offering words of praise to the one we love. God knows that, so he tells us to praise him knowing that love begets praise and praise begets more love. When God asks for our praise and worship, he is inviting us into expressive relationship with him.

If we can't think of any creative ways to praise God, we can begin by reading to him some of David's psalms. Try Psalm 8, 48, 84, 103, and 105. Then we can learn to express to God our love for him and our thankfulness for all that he is to us and for all that he does for us. The praise that we offer to him will enable us to experience in full the joy of our relationship with God. To put it another way, we just may kick up our heels with happiness and say, "Yeah, God!" He likes that kind of response, and so will we.

T U E S D A Y

M e d i t a t i o n

"Praise God, everybody!
Applaud God, all people!
His love has taken over our lives;
God's faithful ways are eternal.
Hallelujah!"
(Psalm 117 *The Message*)

Think about how God's love has taken over your life. Then meditate on what it means to applaud God. Thank him for his eternally faithful ways.

J o u r n a l

W E D N E S D A Y

T h o u g h t s   f o r   t o d a y :

Remember when you first fell in love? You probably drove everyone around you to distraction by talking about your lover all the time. There was only one topic of conversation as far as you were concerned!

The same is true of our relationship with God. When it is good, really good, and growing and wonderful and loving, we want to share it with someone else even if it is just to express our awe of what God is doing for us and our wonder at who he is. Worshipping together with other Christians is a way of sharing in common adoration of the God to whom our affection and praise is directed.

Such unified worship means that, if there are any problems of which we are aware between us and another believer, we must get that problem settled before our worship will be acceptable to God. Jesus instructs in Matthew 5:23–24 that if another believer has something against us and we remember that offense when we begin to worship, we must leave our time of worship and go settle things with our Christian brother or sister before returning to worship. God expects that, whatever the problem between us and another, we will be willing to take the initiative to do all that is possible to settle the issue. Once we experience such unity, we will find that worshipping together strengthens our communion with God and with each other.

THURSDAY

Thoughts for today:

Our acts of worship with other believers are of great importance to God. When there is unity among us, the sense of connection and power in worship is an experience that is not equaled in any other human activity.

When we come together for corporate worship, we are not the audience, God is. It is as if the entire congregation of believers is on stage and God is sitting in the pew waiting for the program to begin. He is the reason we gather. How many times have you heard Christians grumble about a church service, a sermon, or the music? That attitude shows the wrong focus. Our reaction to the service is not what is important. God is the recipient of what we offer as worship in that corporate time; we are the givers, not the receivers. We should never have anything to complain about after a worship service. It is what God thinks of it that really matters!

We can and should worship God in times of devotion when we are alone with him. But we don't want to miss the joy of sharing in praise and worship with other believers. Our worship will be revitalized and broadened by the presence of other worshippers, and our gift of worship to God will be magnified by joining with others who are God's children, too. Worship becomes a party of praise and honor to our great God.

FRIDAY

Reading God's message

Hebrews 10:19–25

Read this passage on worship. What attitudes should we have as we come together to worship? To what end should we be encouraging one another as we worship together? What characteristics of God are emphasized in this passage?

Journal

SATURDAY

For personal reflection

How do you enter into worship with other believers?

_____

_____

What do you enjoy most about worshipping with others who share your love of God?

_____

_____

Are you a part of a church that encourages you to worship freely and whole-heartedly? If not, find a way to become an active participant in worship with other Christians.

Cherish what you have; and enjoy at ever-deepening levels the unity that comes from worshipping God together.

SUNDAY

Prayer

Lord, I'm so happy that you have brought me to a place where I look forward to corporate worship. It used to be drudgery for me—as you well know. Lord, you have lifted off that spirit of heaviness and given me a garment of praise. You did it, Lord, and surprised me again. You are the almighty God, my heavenly Father.

My prayer:

_____

_____

_____

_____

Worshipping Together

P r i n c i p l e   # 45

**Worship is a gift we give to God.
Intimacy and blessings are its rewards.**

Worship is about God and what pleases him. It is about our deep desire to show him how much he means to us. It is elevating God in our hearts and making him the centerpiece of our lives. While the very essence of worship is the focus on God, there are very tangible benefits to us as worshippers.

Worship allows us to experience true joy. As human beings, we are joy seekers. The problem is that we often look for it in places where it really cannot be found. Have you seen the Veggie Tale movie, *Madame Blueberry*? In it, the main character, a very well-do-do, motherly blueberry, loves shopping at Stuff Mart and filling her cart and her home with more and more and more stuff. At the end of the tale she realizes that all the possessions she has accumulated do not bring her happiness. Instead she knows that she should be thankful for what she has and should give up the quest to accumulate more and more. The movie concludes with big, round, blue Madame Blueberry singing a song of awareness in which we hear this line, "A thankful heart is a happy heart."

Expressing our praise and thanksgiving to God in worship allows gratefulness to grow within us, and gratefulness cannot enter our hearts without bringing happiness along with it. We can't have one without the other. Let us recognize that joy is a natural and assured result of our worship times with God. When we are thankful and when we are receiving his love, we will feel genuine joy. It is inevitable.

Worship enables us to know God better. C. S. Lewis once wrote, "It is in the process of being worshipped that God communicates His presence to men" (Collins Clear Type Press, 1961, p. 79). When we worship God, we open ourselves up to receive him, to be filled and controlled by his Spirit, to experience his love, to understand his thoughts, and in these ways to know him in new and intimate ways.

Worship begins to transform us into Christ's image. Have you ever met a couple who, having been married for many, many years, have begun to look alike? We will grow to be like whatever it is that we worship. When we spend minutes, hours, days, and eventually years in worshipful devotion to God, it is inevitable that we will begin to look like him. He will see to it that the transformation happens. What satisfaction when people begin to recognize our heavenly Father in us!

TUESDAY

Meditation

"May the Master pour on the love so it fills your lives and splashes over on everyone around you, just as it does from us to you. May you be infused with strength and purity, filled with confidence in the presence of God our Father... ."
(I Thessalonians 3:12–13 *The Message*)

Meditate on the characteristics that God desires for you as expressed in these verses. Ask the Holy Spirit to reveal to you what part of this passage is most applicable to you today.

Journal

WEDNESDAY

T h o u g h t s   f o r   t o d a y :

Worship releases us from ourselves. The less emotional, physical, and spiritual focus we have on our own beings, the more free we will be of the control demands of the hardest of all taskmasters—ourselves. The only real solution to taking the attention off of us is to give it elsewhere. Our loving God, as the sovereign being in the universe, is the only one who is worthy of our praise and worship and, therefore, the one who should be receiving it. Whenever our focus is directed toward God, he is taking care of us and he does a far better job than we can anyway! So, instead of giving our devotion to our emotional well-being, our financial success, our physical conditioning, or our approval rating, we, through worship, begin to redirect our attention to God. Only then will we be released from the slavery to self that we have experienced all of our lives.

Worship draws us closer to one another. If God is the center of my attention and he also is the center of yours, then you and I are drawn closer together. We share a common interest, a mutual goal, a bond of agreement. Then, as the worship grows within our hearts, that bond grows deeper and more emotionally satisfying. We are one in God's Spirit as we worship him together.

T H U R S D A Y

T h o u g h t s   f o r   t o d a y :

When we engage in worship with our eyes riveted on God, he reaches out to us and graciously meets the deepest needs of our beings. John the Baptist said, "He must become greater, I must become less" (John 3:30). That statement should be the cry of our hearts. If we are trying to enable self to decrease by pushing it down, keeping it under control, and making demands on it, we will not succeed. As soon as we take the focus away from self and away from seeking our own happiness and, instead, turn to God in worship, all other priorities will fall quietly and quickly into place.

How many people do you know who can claim they know God? How many are living a life free of enslavement to their own personalities? How many are consistently experiencing joy? How many feel a true unity with other believers? How many know God in an intimately satisfying way? We offer our worship to God because we know he deserves it and because we love him and want to give this gift to him. We offer it freely and without any expectation of reward. But we find that we cannot give to God more than he gives in return. His gifts of knowledge of himself, freedom to be our true selves, unity with others, and joy unending will set us apart as beloved people living life as God intended it to be lived.

F R I D A Y

R e a d i n g   G o d ' s   m e s s a g e

Psalm 98

What are the reasons for worship that are recounted in this psalm? In what physical ways does the psalmist urge us to worship God? How does he envision creation participating in worship?

J o u r n a l

SATURDAY

F o r   p e r s o n a l   r e f l e c t i o n

Write down what you know already about God, his character, and his activities in the world.

_____

_____

_____

Pray, asking that God will reveal more and more about himself as you spend time in worship.

Then, through the weeks and months to come, add to your list as he answers that prayer.

_____

_____

SUNDAY

P r a y e r

Lord Jesus, you are the lover of my soul; what a joy to be dwelling in your tent, covered with your love and protection. It's cozy in this tent with you, Jesus. The poles are strong and the stakes are secure because you have established it for us so we can spend time together. What better use of my time could there be?

My prayer:

_____

_____

_____

_____

Receiving the Rewards

We Worship a Joyful God

P r i n c i p l e # 46

God loves to celebrate!

If you were to ask a hundred people their purpose in life, they may give multifaceted answers, but most would include the goal of finding personal happiness. Even if happiness is not what we claim to seek, if you look at how Madison Avenue promotes what they want us to purchase, and if you look at the choices we make in our day-to-day lives, you will find that happiness is an objective to which we naturally and almost universally aspire. We want to be happy. We want to experience joy. We want the personal peace and comfort that comes from feeling good. There is nothing wrong with having that desire. God wants us to be joyful, too.

In this world, there are a number of ways to attempt to accomplish that goal. Some men and women turn to work and to personal achievement, others to self-sacrificing service of humanity, others to more obvious comforts such as food, alcohol, sex, drugs, or the pleasures of travel, materialism, and plush surroundings.

Our society is affluent, and many are able to purchase the stuff of which happiness purportedly is made. Yet how many people do you know whom you would describe as happy? Suicide rates are at an all-time high. Treatment of depression is a big business. Psychologists see clients routinely who are just dissatisfied with life and cannot really pinpoint why. This kind of melancholy seems to affect all cross-sections of life, including those who are wealthy and those who are poor, those who have families and those who live in solitude, those who believe in God and those who are agnostic. Why is it that the happiness that is promised by media and sought by our own instincts does not materialize?

The answer is found within us and through our relationship with our God. Scripture tells us that if we want to gain real life, a joyful life, we need to lose the life we have now. We need to stop doing all the things we have historically done in our search for happiness and begin to focus on God, the one who knows better than we ever can what will be truly fulfilling to us. The kind of joy we seek is not dependent upon circumstances, is not dependent upon our own well-being, is not dependent upon our own comfort, lasts forever, and comes from God instead of us.

T U E S D A Y

Meditation

**"When the righteous see God in action
they'll laugh, they'll sing,
they'll laugh and sing for joy.**
(Psalm 68:3 *The Message*)

Meditate on the various evidences of happiness in this verse. Ask God to remind you of ways he has been in action in your life; then be joyful in praise to him.

W E D N E S D A Y

Thoughts for today:

In our study of Scripture, we find that we are to develop the very qualities of God in ourselves. After all, Genesis tells us we have been created in his image; that means that we once shared the characteristics of God. After the fall in the Garden of Eden, those characteristics in mankind were marred, distorted, and diluted, and a separation from God occurred. God made a way through Jesus for reconciliation to take place between us and himself and, in that very reconciliation, made it possible for us to reconnect with the qualities of God that he wants to develop in our lives.

We often hear of God's holiness, his anger toward sin, and his awesome power, but we do not as often hear about the fact that he is a God of celebration and joy. The God who demands purity from sin is also the God who established seven major celebrations for the nation of Israel to hold each year. These were parties that lasted for several days, and the joyful eating and sharing among entire communities was accompanied by singing and dancing and just plain fun. God wanted his people to enjoy the blessings he had given, to acknowledge from whom those pleasures had come, and to party in celebration. He wanted that so much, that he actually commanded them to do it. God wants us to be happy!

THURSDAY

Thoughts for today:

The value of celebration is illustrated in the book of Nehemiah. Many Israelites who had been taken as prisoners of war had been held captive in Babylon for many years. At the time of Nehemiah, a number of them had been released and had returned to Jerusalem to rebuild its walls and restore the temple. In that process, they discovered an old scroll of God's law and began to read it. As they read, they wept, realizing how far away from God and his requirements they had drifted during their captivity.

Nehemiah stopped them in the middle of this somber religious service and told the people to quit crying and, instead, to take a break and put on a party. He promised that the joy they experienced in the celebration would give them strength—strength to face the message that God was communicating and to move forward in their obedient relationship with him.

Yes, God demands purity, confession of sins, and personal sacrifice. Our Christian lives are not all fun and games. But God balances the seriousness of our relationship with him with an opportunity to express the joy that such a relationship brings. Sometimes even during our solemn recognition of how far we fall short of God's desires for us, he calls for celebration. He enjoys us and wants us to enjoy him. Joy is a part of God's very character, and he wants to make it part of ours, too.

FRIDAY

Reading God's message

Nehemiah 8

Read for yourself the story of the reading of the law in Nehemiah. Witness the importance of celebration and joy and the refreshment and strength it gave to God's people.

Journal

SATURDAY

For   personal   reflection

What kinds of things do you think would bring joy to the heart of God?

_____

_____

Why is he a happy being?

_____

_____

What characteristics might God desire to develop in you so that you can share in his joys? Ask him; make a list of what he may reveal to you.

_____

_____

SUNDAY

Prayer

Hallelujah! Jesus is alive! The sheer joy of knowing that truth brings new life into me, Father. Let this new life coming from the source of resurrected life spill over into my world. You have made me to be a fountain of life; keep me bubbling up and splashing on everyone I meet. What fun we have together!

My prayer:

_____

_____

_____

_____

We Worship a Joyful God

P r i n c i p l e # 47

God came to earth to let us know that our happiness is very important to him.

Joy is not something we selfishly pursue, but when we pursue God, he gives it freely as a gift. Galatians 5:22 lists joy as a fruit of the Spirit. When the Holy Spirit is dwelling in us and we are yielding our lives and our selves to his control, joy will result. When we give up control, focus on our relationship with God, and allow him to transform us, joy is promised. God wants it for us more than we want it for ourselves. The difference is that he knows better than we do what it takes for us to be truly joyful.

We sometimes think we know what will make us happy; so, instead of believing that God's plan for our joy will work, we find all sorts of ways to try to go around God and find it for ourselves—only to fail miserably every time. Let's give up being miserable and open the pathways between us and God so that joy can flow through from his heart to ours.

What did the angel say to the shepherds when he announced the coming of the Christ child? "I bring you good news of great joy that will be for all the people" (Luke 2:10b). The coming of the Messiah was a signal of joy. Things would change in the world now. The sorrow, the pain, the agony of sin and man's inhumanity to man would be redeemed. There would be purpose to it. There would be release from it. There would be another way.

Now, fast forward to the last supper that Jesus had with his disciples before he was killed and let's listen to the summation of his teachings to them. He says, in John 15:10–11, "I have told you this so that my joy may be in you and that your joy may be complete." Later, in John 16:22, Jesus tells them, "… I will see you again and you will rejoice, and no one will take away our joy… Ask and you will receive, and your joy will be complete."

Just think of it! He came heralded by an angel announcing joy. He left this world stating that his final purpose was to fulfill the joy of those who chose to follow him through obedience. Is there any doubt that joy was a very important part of Jesus' earthly mission?

TUESDAY

Meditation

"I've told you these things for purpose: that my joy might be your joy, and your joy wholly mature."
(Words of Jesus to his disciples on the night he was to be arrested and killed. John 15:11 *The Message*)

Ponder what Jesus meant by mature joy. Spend time meditating on Jesus' desire that we experience the kind of joy he has. How might that look in your life?

Journal

WEDNESDAY

Thoughts for today:

By the time Jesus and his disciples had their last supper together, they had left their homes and families, abandoned their careers, and wandered from place to place followed by motley crowds from morning until night. Then they were sent out to preach the Gospel, which very few really wanted to hear.

Yet, the angels said that Jesus came to bring joy and he left this world stating that his desire for them was that their joy be completed. Was this joy just wishful thinking? No. Joy and fulfillment are among God's greatest desires for us. He knows that true joy is found in following him, in serving others, and in finding meaning in life through keeping our eyes on eternal rewards.

Did Jesus' promise of joy become a reality in the lives of the disciples? When we read the later writings of John and Peter we realize that, although they experienced suffering in this life, inexplicable joy accompanied it. Not only that, the disciples lived this life looking forward to another world—the final fulfillment of Jesus' promises to them.

There was joy in the journey of life and joy in anticipation of all that was yet to come. The same promises are given for us today. There is an eternal joy that we will not experience in fullness until we are with Jesus in heaven.

THURSDAY

Thoughts for today:

Once we have been adopted into God's family, we are guaranteed to receive an inheritance from our heavenly Father, and that inheritance includes eternal life with him in heaven (Ephesians 1:14). It's a done deal.

When we know that our future is secure, the day-to-day struggles of life take on a new perspective. What used to terrify us no longer has power over us. The fear of failure, fear of financial ruin, fear of sickness, and fear of death have no hold on us. God has redeemed us, he holds us close to his heart, and he is someday taking us to eternal glory in the heavens where no insecurity will ever again haunt us. Because God says that our future is guaranteed, and because we have learned that he is 100 percent trustworthy, our joy transcends any earthly problem or fear that we may face.

And here is the crowning message the Bible gives us about joy. We are confident that when we show up in heaven, we will know true and everlasting happiness, but Jude 24 tells us that God presents us "before his glorious presence without fault and with great joy… ." Our being there will bring God joy! Doesn't that thought just thrill you down to your toes? He is not just fulfilling an obligation in letting us into his heaven, he *wants* us there. He loves us that much. We bring him joy.

FRIDAY

Reading God's message

John 16

This passage records the concluding words of Jesus to his disciples just before he was arrested and killed. A person's last words are always considered to be of great significance. Take note of the focus of the message that Jesus felt was most important for his disciples to remember in the coming days.

Journal

SATURDAY

For personal reflection

Think of ways that you can disconnect from constant work and pressure and take mini-vacations of celebration. In other words, how can you learn to enjoy your life more?

_____

_____

How can you learn to enjoy the God of celebration more?

_____

Remember what anticipation of Christmas morning felt like to you when you were about ten years old? Let that same excitement seep into your very being as you think about living forever in heaven with God, enjoying him and all his other children forever and ever. Spend time reflecting upon what heaven will be like.

Thank your heavenly Father for preparing such a wonderful future for you!

SUNDAY

Prayer

Jesus, thank you for coming as a baby. Every time I see a baby, it reminds me of your unconditional love. Help me to have that childlike quality of open and honest love, the love that doesn't hold back or hide, the love that flows out of a child's heart and makes people smile and feel warm inside. It's a cold world, Father, and I want more of the warmth of your love and joy. I ask for it in Jesus' powerful, loving name. Amen.

My prayer:

_____

_____

_____

_____

God Wants You to Be Happy

P r i n c i p l e # 48

Joy sneaks up when you least expect it.

Joy is one of those elusive qualities that escapes us when we seek it. If we are looking for joy, we are selfishly motivated, and that very selfishness will cause happiness to be hard to find. Psychologists tell us that depression is defined by a self-focus, a turning inward, and a feeling of hopeless isolation. Joy, on the other hand, comes to us when we are not focused on ourselves, when we are, instead, following Christ and serving others. Thomas Merton, in his book *New Seeds of Contemplation*, says, "...perfect joy is possible only when we have completely forgotten ourselves" (New Directions Publishing Corp., 1952, p. 58). How do we forget ourselves? We certainly cannot do it by concentration or self-discipline. Self-forgetfulness comes only when we are following steps of simple obedience, trust, and commitment to growth.

When we begin each day in communion with our heavenly Father, with open hearts listening to his directions to us for the day, and when we receive his love in order to give it away to others we meet, joy sneaks in. It is just there! But it will not be coerced or forced. It comes unbidden when we are the least likely to be looking for it.

The choice we make to focus on God and others instead of our selves will give us new insight into the source of true joy in our lives. For example, from our human perspective, we think that if we are going to be happy, we must be enjoying a trouble-free life. God's perspective is diametrically opposed to that. In chapter one of his epistle, James says, "Consider it pure joy, my brothers, whenever you face trials of many kinds, because you know that the testing of your faith develops perseverance. Perseverance must finish its work so that you may be mature and complete, not lacking anything." James says to consider it all joy. That's a command.

James does not command our feelings, but he does tell us that if we are sincere Christ followers, we will consider and, in fact, call it joy when we have problems. Is choosing joy our natural human tendency? No. Emotionally, we may feel drained; we may be experiencing fear or guilt or anger. But James says to receive our troubles with joy—that seems to be in direct contradiction to what we would naturally do. We are simply told to make a choice: Choose joy.

TUESDAY

M e d i t a t i o n

"We continue to shout our praise even when we're hemmed in with troubles, because we know how troubles can develop passionate patience in us, and how that patience, in turn, forges the tempered steel of virtue, keeping us alert for whatever God will do next.
(Romans 5:3–4 *The Message*)

Meditate on the idea of being full of praise even in times of difficulty. Ponder what God may be doing in your life through troubles that you face.

J o u r n a l

WEDNESDAY

T h o u g h t s   f o r   t o d a y :

There are times when our faith is tested and we have a choice to make. If we are committed to the way of the Spirit, we simply choose to trust God. The same goes for joy. We can choose it or we can choose to follow our waffling feelings.

Paul, the apostle, is a perfect example of joy in the middle of trouble. Today, when we look back on Paul's life, we hold him in high regard as we honor him for his faithfulness to God, his truthful teaching of God's message to the early believers, and his tenacity in the face of severe trials. But let's try to imagine life as Paul saw it. He had been a member of the Sanhedrin, the highest ruling Jewish council. He had been educated by the best of Hebrew teachers and, therefore, we can conclude that he came from an upstanding and prosperous Jewish family.

After his conversion, that life of privilege was over. He was outcast from all those who had looked up to him before he became a Christ follower. He became an itinerate missionary going from city to city in the Mediterranean areas preaching the message of Christ and, many times, being smuggled away to avoid being killed. Paul had every reason to feel down. Yet, when we read his writings, we find that joy was one of his primary themes.

T H U R S D A Y

T h o u g h t s   f o r   t o d a y :

Many who heard Paul believed what he preached, but a greater number of people simply thought he was insane. He must have wondered that himself at times! He is even criticized by the early believers and ridiculed by other traveling preachers. He endured all kinds of trials and faced many obstacles to the work he was called to do.

Probably Paul would have preferred a comfortable life, respect from his fellow believers, and honor from his Jewish friends. When he was writing, traveling, and teaching in A.D. 60, he could not have comprehended how influential he would be on the establishment of the church and on our understanding of God and spiritual truths today. Instead, he saw the struggles that he faced day by day. There is no reason that Paul should have felt at that time anything but discouragement and depression.

Yet he writes to the Corinthians, "…in all our troubles my joy knows no bounds" (7:4b). In his letter to the Philippians, he says, "Rejoice in the Lord always. I will say it again: Rejoice!" (4:4). To the Thessalonians, he writes, "Be joyful always. . ." (5:16), and to the Romans, "May the God of hope fill you with all joy…" (15:13). Joy would not have flowed naturally out of the life he was living. But joy was a gift from God that overtook Paul right in the middle of his troubles.

F R I D A Y

R e a d i n g   G o d ' s   m e s s a g e

II Corinthians 11:24–12:10

Read in this passage all that Paul suffered as a follower of Christ. What is his attitude through it all?

J o u r n a l

SATURDAY

For personal reflection

Is there an area of your life about which you need to choose joy?

_____

_____

_____

Do you trust God enough to allow him to fill you with joy in the middle of negative circumstances? This does not mean that you minimize your troubles or neglect to deal with them. This is not denial—this is a conscious choice to have joy no matter how bad your situation is.

Tell God that you choose joy. If you cannot, ask him to enable you to make that choice to his glory.

SUNDAY

Prayer

Jesus, you are the earthly representation of my heavenly Father. You came that I might know the joy of family relationship with God, the almighty one, the most high God. Through this gift to me, you have given me the power to make choices that are according to your will. Lord, I give my will to you so that I may come closer, and live in the house of your heart where there is joy everlasting. Give me your picture of joy. I ask in Jesus' name. Amen.

My prayer:

_____

_____

_____

_____

Joy is a Choice

P r i n c i p l e # 49

The true joy of God meets our deepest soul-needs.

Choosing joy in the middle of our troubles is not an irrational decision. It is, instead, one that is rooted in our trust in God, who provides us with a foundation and security that those around us do not have. As we think about all the joys that are ours once we are rightly related to God, we realize this supernatural joy is consistent even in the face of trials and struggles in this earthly life.

First there is...

The joy of forgiveness. R. C. Sproul, in one of his taped teachings, says that when he talks to agnostics or atheists and they present their arguments about the nonexistence of God, he tries to convince them of the necessity of God. When unsuccessful in his argument, he turns to the debater and says, "So, without God, what do you do with your guilt?" (Ligonier Ministries, 1966, vol. 6). The question always brings the person up short because, outside of God, there is no answer for the universal problem of human guilt. On the other hand, we as Christians can live guilt-free lives. Our sins are forgiven, the guilt of our past is expunged, and as long as we respond with confession when the Holy Spirit convicts us of sins of the present, there is no cause for us to carry any guilt. In Psalm 51, when David repents of his sin, he asks that God restore the joy of his salvation. With forgiveness comes renewed relationship with God and revitalized joy.

Forgiveness is a topic that relates not only to the relationship between us and God but to us and other humans as well. As believers walking close to God, we forgive those who have offended or hurt us. A great deal of money is spent each year for psychologists and psychiatrists because people harbor bitterness, resentment, and unforgiveness. These feelings are a huge burden to bear. If we are Christ followers, however, we do not have to bear that burden because, by the grace of God and out of sheer thanksgiving for his forgiveness for us, we forgive our brothers and sisters and are free of the bitter, angry spirit that accompanies unforgiveness. If you have ever experienced the renewed energy that overwhelms a person who has finally been able to forgive an offending party, you know that. Once the bitterness is gone, joy fills the space. The change is evident by a smiling face, a lightness of body, and overflowing joy.

TUESDAY

Meditation

"He brings gifts into our lives, much the same way that fruit appears in an orchard—things like affection for others, exuberance about life, serenity."
(Galatians 5:22a *The Message*)

Ponder how each of these three characteristics evidences itself in your life. Meditate on the gift that you believe God wants to grow more fully in you: Is it love, joy, or peace?

Journal

WEDNESDAY

Thoughts for today:

The joy of peace. If we practice the things we have been studying together, we will live lives that are free of anxiety because we will be applying Philippians 4:6–7 which tells us not to worry about anything, but to pray about everything. Stress becomes a thing of the past for the committed, growing Christian. Instead of being worried, we pray. Think of the joy that comes from giving our stress over to someone who can really do something about all that concerns us. God gives us a new perspective on what it is that troubles us. He removes the anxiety and supernaturally replaces it with peace.

The joy of serving. As we walk with God we find ourselves reaching out more and more to others. Our love for those around us will grow, the compassionate heart of God will begin to beat in us, and we will feel compelled to help those in need. It may be as simple as giving directions to a family who is looking for Applebee's. Or it may be working on a crew building a house for Habitat for Humanity, serving soup at the local rescue mission, taking in a foster child, or going to a foreign country to do missionary work. Whatever way we choose to serve, we need to know that our newly opened eyes will see need and will want to serve. The unsought reward for selfless service is joy.

THURSDAY

Thoughts for today:

The joy of transformed minds. Our lives are transformed by the renewal of our minds (Romans 12:2). When we focus on God and choose to follow him, we choose personal growth, mind-boggling truth, and supernatural change, all of which allow us to relate closer and more fully to the God who loves us and shares his joy with us.

The joy of humility. Thomas Merton in his book *New Seeds of Contemplation* says this about living a life of humility: "In humility is the greatest freedom. As long as you have to defend the imaginary self that you think is important, you lose your peace of heart. As soon as you compare that shadow with the shadows of other people, you lose all joy, because you have begun to trade in unrealities, and there is no joy in things that do not exist" (New Directions Publishing Corp., 1962, p. 57).

As Christians, we begin to see the truth about ourselves, and seeing ourselves as God sees us is a very good definition of humility. When we are humble, we do not have to defend ourselves, we are not easily offended, we are not seeking our own best interest, and we are not hung up on issues of self-esteem. Instead, we lose sight of ourselves and reach out to God and to others in love. The practice of true humility frees us from the encumbrances of protecting our self-created images and, in that freedom, we experience joy.

FRIDAY

Reading God's message

Psalm 4

What problems is David facing in this psalm? What verses or phrases show his willingness to give his problems over to God? What is his attitude by the time he concludes this psalm?

Journal

SATURDAY

For personal reflection

Have you accepted the forgiveness that God offers? Not just forgiveness that gets you into his kingdom, but forgiveness of the
- sins that hurt others and you wish you could go back and change.
- sins that you keep committing over and over in spite of confession.
- sins that you would never tell another human being.

Tell all to God. Confess your sin and accept the cleansing forgiveness that he died to give you.

Which of the evidences of joy discussed this week is strong in your life?

_____

Which is weak?

_____

Pray, asking God to fill you with his supernatural joy so that your joy overflows into every area of your life. In faith, accept that he will answer your prayer and then watch for joy to creep in—even in unexpected places!

SUNDAY

Prayer

Lord, you took my anger and gave me joy. You took my misery and gave me acceptance. Lord, when did you do this? It changed my life from dark to light. Once I was lost and now I am found. You call it the exchanged life. You got death and I got freedom and life. What a way to live! Show me what else I am hanging onto that is waiting to be exchanged and I will sing even more new songs of praise unto my God.

My prayer:

_____

_____

_____

_____

Experience Joy-filled Living

P r i n c i p l e # 50

It's far easier to love mankind than it is to love the human beings who share our daily lives!

We live in a world that likes to speak of balance. We balance exercise with rest, work with play, achievement with reward, overeating with dieting, self-discipline with pleasure, and the spiritual with the temporal. After all, the balanced life is what we are looking for, isn't it? Maybe not. Maybe it's time to throw away the concept of balance and allow the Spirit of God to lead us to radical living that will bring glory to God, will give us full and vital satisfaction as we live in this world, and will reap eternal benefits for his kingdom. Let's look together at what a life that is totally committed to God might look like and how radical it might be perceived in the world around us.

Jesus rocked the Jewish world when, in what we now call the Sermon on Mount (Matthew 5–7), he gave relationship directives that include

- loving our enemies,
- praying for those who persecute us,
- not turning away from one who wants to borrow from us,
- giving to the needy,
- forgiving those who sin against us, and
- withholding judgment of others.

Loving enemies is hard for us today, but it was really radical back in Jesus' time when the enemies were cruel Roman soldiers who required more and more from the conquered Jews. "Love them," Jesus said. "Give more than they ask of you. Forgive them."

He wanted his followers to go back to the basics, to the roots in human relationship that were there even before the law was given. The law was given to govern people's behavior—to keep them from killing each other, lying, stealing, and committing adultery. Jesus' teaching went back earlier than the law to the heart of the matter. He was interested in relationships based on heart attitudes, not just based on outward behavior. In fact, in a later teaching, Jesus summed up the entire law system by saying in Matthew 22:37–39, "Love the Lord your God with all your heart and with all your soul and with all your mind. This is the first and greatest commandment. And the second is like it: 'Love your neighbor as yourself.'" I had a pastor when I was in college who used to say that when we stand before Christ in judgment, he will have only one question for us about our time on earth and that is, "How was your love life?"

TUESDAY

Meditation

"Real wisdom, God's wisdom, begins with a holy life and is characterized by getting along with others. It is gentle and reasonable, overflowing with mercy and blessings... ."
(James 3:17 *The Message*)

Meditate on the characteristics of God's wisdom. Ask God to reveal to you how he would like that wisdom to show itself in the way you treat others.

Journal

WEDNESDAY

Thoughts for today:

Do our present lives reflect that we love God with all our hearts? The test of our love, according to Jesus' teaching, is our obedience. If we love him, obedience to his commands will never be a problem. Augustine was so confident of that fact that he said, "Love God and do what you please." With that kind of love commitment, we will look at scriptural passages, read the commands, and then, no matter what is going in our lives at that moment, we will say, "OK, God. I will do what you want. I will obey." A good test of our love toward God might be to go through a chapter of the Bible and list the commands that we read. If these are commands given by God, it seems that we should take them very seriously.

Yet, how many times have we said to God,

- "I would do that, but...it doesn't work for me," or
- "You don't understand the situation I am in right now," or
- "If I had a different husband (or wife, or home, or job), I could do this."

Loving the Lord our God with all our hearts means we say, "OK, God. You said it and I will do it out of love for you and, if necessary, at a personal sacrifice of myself and my own needs in order to be obedient to you."

THURSDAY

Thoughts for today:

Love also needs to rule our relationships with other people. God's definition of the practice of that kind of love involves
- putting the other persons first,
- seeking their best interests,
- sacrificing for them,
- forgiving them no matter what they have done,
- always seeing the best in them, and
- never giving up on them.

   Biblical love is not manipulative or controlling; instead it seeks the best for the other person without regard to our own needs. That is radical love and rare in the world today! A well known, biblical description of love is found, as we read in Week 34, in I Corinthians 13. How many people in your life are you willing or able to love that way?

   Simply applying the forgiveness principle will cause others to think we have lost our good sense. In today's world we find these rules practiced: If someone offends you, sue. If someone cheats on you, report them to the regulatory agencies. If someone lies about you, defend yourself and announce publicly the dirt you have on them. If your spouse commits adultery, divorce him/her. If, instead, we follow God's way, we will be perceived as being radical, but the biblical path is the way we are empowered to live. Love, forgive, give, give, give, lay down your life, love, care, share, serve, give, love, forgive... .

FRIDAY

Reading God's message

Ephesians 5

As you read this chapter, write down all the commands you find. What specific instructions does God give us for treating other people?

Journal

SATURDAY

F o r   p e r s o n a l   r e f l e c t i o n

If you are going to live a God-centered life, how does your attitude toward others have to change?

_____

_____

_____

Ask God to soften your heart toward others (give him specific names if they come to mind), to allow you to see them as he does, to enable you to love them as he does, and to grow you until you can show that love even to those who are most unlovable.

_____

_____

_____

SUNDAY

P r a y e r

Lord, you and I get along fine. It's these other people that you invite into our tent that I have problems with. Maybe when I understand that there cannot be community without conflict, I will be more open to this. Please continually remind me that there is enough of your love for all who will come to you. You have a well that never runs dry. I can come and draw out whatever I need, anytime I need it. Assure me, my Savior, of your never-ending presence. I can never be separated from your love.

My prayer:

_____

_____

_____

Radical Relationships

Time in Light of Eternity

P r i n c i p l e   # 51

Have the time of your life! But do so in light of the eternity of your life.

The concept of time takes on an entirely new meaning when we are living a God-centered life. Time is a commodity that we use until it runs out; then we move into eternity, which is timeless and endless. Many teachings of the Bible, however, indicate that the quality of our eternal life depends to a great extent on the use of our time on earth. So we don't want to just let time pass; instead, we choose to spend it, use it, and invest it into the eternity that goes on and on forever. To us, time that is not taking eternity into account is wasted time.

Does that mean we never relax, never just "hang out" with friends? No. Building friendships, renewing our souls, and re-energizing our bodies are all important in light of eternity. Besides, God says that he wants us to enjoy this life, so it's not that we have to be busy all of the time. But whatever we do with the time we have, we must do it keeping in mind God's eternal perspective.

With that perspective, we will find that we live more in the moment, we are attuned to his direction for the time in front of us right now, we are flexible to change of direction at his nudging, and we are not frantically trying to accomplish more than a human being can do. Our time becomes God's commodity and not ours. We don't have to be responsible to produce a certain number of widgets or souls, as the case may be. We just have to give God this particular moment and allow him to use the time that we have. He will accomplish through us all that he has in mind for us to do in any given day.

What a relief! Time becomes our friend, our tool, and effective for God's kingdom work when we give it to him. We stop seeing time as the enemy because of its fleeting nature, and we rest from our frenzied efforts to fill it to the maximum. We tend to measure ourselves by our accomplishments and feel that the harder we work, the more we will achieve. God measures things differently. It may be just one conversation we have today that will count immeasurably for eternity, but it may be a conversation we would never have had if we had not committed our time to God and were not living fully connected to him.

TUESDAY

Meditation

"The things we see now are here today gone tomorrow. But the things we can't see now will last forever."
(II Corinthians 4:18 *The Message*)

Think about the "things we can't see" that God says will last forever. Ask God to open your eyes to eternity and to the values he wants you to be living for during your earthly life.

Journal

WEDNESDAY

Thoughts for today:

While we are in this world, we have to protect our time from being stolen by others, by our own need for approval from people, and by our desire to achieve; then we can focus on what God wants to do in the moment in front of us. If we set these priorities, we will be able to pray at the end of our lives as Jesus did in John 17:4, "I have brought you glory on earth by completing the work you gave me to do." I would rather pray that prayer than to try to explain to God that I was getting around to his assignments just as soon as I had finished washing the car.

Also, as we focus on eternity, we begin to feel less at home in this world. Life on this earth was originally created in perfection, but what was made originally has been distorted by the sinful nature of mankind and by the forces of evil that represent Satan, the father of lies. As a result, we find that the life of truth that Christ has called us to live will not coincide with the life that our culture is purporting as normal. So we should not be surprised that we often do not feel comfortable with the world's standards. Our discomfort proves that we belong to a better world, a world of truth and light, created as our eternal home.

THURSDAY

T h o u g h t s   f o r   t o d a y :

We must direct our minds and hearts to the real world, which is the world of the spirit. That world is eternal, it is the very embodiment of truth and reality, and it is centered around God himself. It is more real and has more substance than any earthly world we can touch and see today.

But in adopting the real-world focus, we will become misfits in this temporal world. Our God-centered living flies in the face of cultural values and everything that seems sensible and right in this earthly world. As Peter says, we are "aliens and strangers in the world" (I Peter 2:11). We have to be strong enough to judge our choices by God's word and to determine for ourselves which of the things of this world we have to turn our backs on and which we can embrace.

Not everything in this world is wrong or evil. God has created this world and has populated it with people, many of whom belong to him and have influenced the society of today with the truth that they know and have experienced. We must be wise in our choices, willing to go against the status quo, and committed enough to determine to go God's way even when his way is counter to the cultural norm. Those choices will be the measure of our commitment to God's eternal values.

FRIDAY

R e a d i n g   G o d ' s   m e s s a g e

I Peter 2:9–25

Read this passage, taking note of the life instructions Peter gives. What does he say that indicates we have an allegiance that is greater than our allegiance to this world? How should we live in relationship to others in this world?

J o u r n a l

SATURDAY

For personal reflection

What do you spend time on that will not last beyond this life?

_____

_____

Ask God to reveal activities and time-users in your life that you must abandon in order to focus on the eternal values that he defines. Know that his eternal values will bring ultimate purpose and satisfaction to both this life and the everlasting life to come. Write them here:

_____

_____

Do you sometimes feel disconnected with the world around you? Have you ever thought that it is because you have a higher calling? A real home that is not in this world? Thank God for giving you a purpose in life that reaches beyond the shallowness of the world around you and ask him to reveal that purpose and direction to you one step at a time.

SUNDAY

Prayer

Father, can eternity be true? This joy and happiness of living and walking with you every day will never end? I only have to take it one day at a time, but each day I am walking closer to your home. Father, God, I so desire to fulfill my destiny; walk it out with me and let me celebrate our life together every day. I need your grace to daily choose life and to keep growing up into the head of the body which is Jesus. He fills everything everywhere with himself! Glory be to you, O Lord!

My prayer:

_____

_____

_____

Time in Light of Eternity

P r i n c i p l e # 52

We don't know how exhilarating it is to fly until we take off!

C. S. Lewis said this of his love for Joy Davidman in *A Grief Observed*, which was written in the period of mourning her death: "We want to prove to ourselves that we are lovers on a grand scale, tragic heroes; not just ordinary privates in the huge army of the bereaved, slogging along and making the best of a bad job" (Bantam Books, 1961, p. 63).

I think we agree that we don't want to be ordinary privates in the army of God, either. We want to be Green Berets, soldiers who are willing to risk our lives and our all for the Commander-in-Chief, fighters not content with merely putting in time, but in living with the goal of triumph and eventually enjoying the fruits of victory after a fight well fought, and after a life well lived.

What kind of changes can we expect in our lives if we have such lofty desires and if we are willing to put in the time it takes to evidence the total commitment that we have to God? We have spent considerable time together talking about cultivating our relationship with God. We have touched on the basics of faith, trust, obedience, moment-by-moment living, commitment, faithfulness, worship, truth, and joy. We have returned to the basics of the simple Christian life in order to discover an accurate understanding of how God wants to relate to us. Now, what evidence will we have that the relationship with God that we desire is actually developing?

Galatians 5:22 tells us what spiritual fruit we can expect in our lives if we are connected to the Holy Spirit: "...love, joy, peace, patience, kindness, goodness, faithfulness, gentleness and self-control." This fruit is the promised result of a life committed to God, trusting him, remaining faithful to him, and growing in relationship to him. When we do those things, the fruit is guaranteed to appear. It will come not by our willpower, not by the strength of our desire, not by our setting and achieving of goals—but from God himself.

The bigger the spiritual fruit grows, the more evident it becomes in our lives both to us and to others. We will, without direct effort on our parts, grow to be more loving, more joyful, more patient, kinder, better, more faithful, more gentle and more self-controlled. Only God, through the Holy Spirit, can produce this fruit in our lives; and he has promised to do so if we stay rooted in him.

TUESDAY

Meditation

"And I ask him that with both feet planted firmly on love, you'll be able to take in with all Christians the extravagant dimensions of Christ's love. Reach out and experience the breadth! Test its length! Plumb the depths! Rise to the heights! Live full lives, full in the fullness of God."
(Ephesians 3:18–19 *The Message*)

Meditate on the extravagant love of Christ. Allow the Holy Spirit to fill your heart with his love and to allow you to feel it to the depths of your being. Sit quietly in his presence and let him hug you.

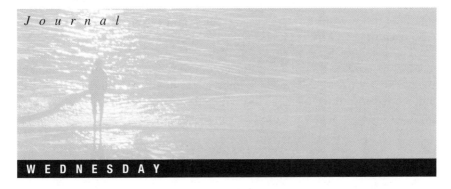

Journal

WEDNESDAY

Thoughts for today:

We have talked a lot about staying focused on our relationship with God and about the kinds of things we can do in terms of Bible reading, prayer, meditation, and spiritual practices that will enable us to grow in relationship with him. Let's not get tired! Let's not give up now! We have come this far and now I want to let you in on a secret that you will eventually discover for yourself. The work we do requires faithfulness, persistence, and commitment, but the real work of growing us up in him and enabling us, as his little eaglets, to spread our wings and fly is up to God!

Sometimes we get discouraged because we are not seeing the progress that we want to see. Sometimes God seems far away and we wonder if we have lost our connection with him. Sometimes we fail God and give in to temptation. Sometimes we are just plain weak and are easily distracted by things around us. But we can take heart from God's promises. They assure us that God never gets tired, that he gives strength to us when we are exhausted, and he restores our power when we are weak. That is the secret to a lifelong relationship with God: When our strength fades, his power is transferred to us and we are re-energized. We just wait quietly with him until we are strong again.

THURSDAY

Thoughts for today:

Our hope for the future, our hope for personal growth, our hope for security and sustenance, our hope for meaning in life, our hope for an eternity in heaven are all placed in the loving hands of God. Once we have placed our hope in God, we wait. Then, all at once, sometimes when we least feel up to it, we take spiritual flight! We soar on wings like eagles'. We find that we are strong! We can swoop and fly and play in the great sky of God. We know more than we thought we knew. We have more power than we realized we had. We have grown more than we thought we had. And now, we are rising to heights we never even knew existed! We are flying!

God teaches us during the waiting times, during the hoping times, during the quiet times, during the purifying times, and during the stressful times. And eventually, we fly. It's all because of him. It's all due to his great love for us and his far-reaching grace.

We don't want to miss it. Let's not stop short of learning to fly. We must be patient and consistent. We need to love God with all our hearts, minds, souls and strength. And we wait on God with a devotion that will allow us, in his perfect timing, to soar on wings like eagles'.

FRIDAY

Reading God's message

Isaiah 40:28–31

Read through these verses several times. Whose strength do we draw on? What promises are given? Who can claim those promises?

Journal

SATURDAY

For personal reflection

Have you inspected the fruit of your relationship with God lately?

How are you doing in developing the characteristics listed in the teaching of this principle?

_____

_____

Recommit yourself to God and invite him to do whatever pruning and watering necessary to grow the fruit of the Spirit described in Galatians 5:22.

Thank God for his faithfulness to you and his desire for you to be intimate with him.

Recommit to him and to placing your hope in him as he renews you, loves you, and enables you to know the total experience of soaring in relationship with him.

SUNDAY

Prayer

O, Lord, you have given me wings so that I can fly away and be at rest. You are my escape and shelter from the stormy wind and tempest. You have given me the power through my sanctified imagination to go anywhere I desire. I fly with you, Lord Jesus, because you are not limited. Thank you for the in-dwelling Holy Spirit who frees me to practice being carried on the wings of an eagle. What a trip you are, Lord; a never-ending adventure. The excitement only grows. You are never dull or boring. Thank you for keeping me a humble learner. I love you back, Jesus. You are the way that I have chosen to go.

My prayer:

_____

_____

_____

Reaping the Results of the God-Centered Life

Epilogue

Some of you may have picked up this book, began to read, and found the message strange and the goals unattainable. There may be a reason for that. The instructions in this book are based on teachings taken from the Bible and are geared toward those who already know God but desire a closer, life-changing walk with him. If you have not become a child of God, then his book, the Bible, may be a mystery to you, and therefore you might believe that the God-sensical lifestyle we described in this book is out of reach.

But if, as you read, you sensed a desire in your heart to be rightly related to God, please follow that desire. It is the urging of the Holy Spirit upon your life drawing you to God. Don't ignore it. Instead, pray. Simply talk to God. Tell him that you realize you have been trying to live your life on your own and that you have left him out entirely. Tell him that you acknowledge that he is the sovereign God who has control over the universe and over your destiny and, therefore, has the right to have control of your life. Tell him that you are sinful but that you claim the payment that Jesus Christ made for your sin when he died on the cross and rose again three days later. Thank him for the forgiveness of sin that Jesus' great gift gives and ask him to apply that forgiveness to you. Then just listen. Pause in his presence and enjoy knowing that your sincere prayer is your way of receiving the gift of salvation and adoption into the family of God. Thank him.

Now tell God that, from this day forward, you are committed to a growing relationship with him through the study of the Bible, through the practice of consistent prayer, and through the fellowship of others who are already Christ followers. Ask that he teach you and promise to allow him to be in control of your life.

It's that simple. Once you have had a conversation like this with the God of the universe, you have turned your face toward him. As long as you keep looking in his direction, and obey the leadings of the Holy Spirit, he will draw you closer and closer to himself and your life, I promise, will radically change!

The choice of making this commitment or not making it is yours alone. A rich, fulfilling, spiritually-rewarding life awaits you if you turn your face toward God. I hope you make the choice to follow him.

My GodSense Life

I choose to follow God.

I learn to know and accept truth.

I am being changed from within.

I trust God.

I live in this moment.

I believe God and act on that belief.

I communicate with God.

I worship my Creator.

I have discovered joy.

I live a meaning-filled life.

Bibliography

Eldredge, John. *The Journey of Desire*. Nashville, Tennessee: Thomas Nelson, Inc., 2000.

Lawrence, Brother. *The Practice of the Presence of God*. Grand Rapids, Michigan: Spire Books, a division of Baker Book House Company, 1967.

Lewis, C. S., *A Grief Observed*. New York, New York: Bantam Books, Inc. by arrangement with The Seabury Press, Inc., 1961.

Lewis, C. S., *Reflections on the Psalms*. London, Great Britain: Collins Clear-Type Press, 1961.

Merton, Thomas. *New Seeds of Contemplation*. New York, New York: New Directions Publishing Corporation, 1962.

Miller, J. Keith. *The Secret Life of the Soul*. Nashville, Tennessee: Broadman & Holman Publishers, 1997.

Sproul, R.C., Foundations. *An Overview of Systematic Theology*. Orlando, Florida: Ligonier Ministries, 1966, Volume 6.

Vanauken, Sheldon. *A Severe Mercy*. New York, New York: HarperCollins Publishers, Inc., 1980.

Veggie Tales. *Madame Blueberry*. Chicago, Illinois: Big Idea Productions, Inc., 1993.

Vernick, Leslie. *How to Live Right When Your Life Goes Wrong*. Colorado Springs, Colorado: Waterbrook Press, 2003.

About the Author

Beverly Van Kampen is a freelance writer and Bible teacher. A former journalist, she has a bachelor's degree in journalism and education from Central Michigan University and is semi-retired from a successful business career. Van Kampen lives in Spring Lake, Michigan, with her husband, Warren.

and her collaborator:

Margery Lembke, who created the fifty-two prayers that appear in this devotional, has been involved in prayer ministry within the body of Christ for more than 25 years. She serves as Prayer Coordinator at Lakeshore Lutheran Fellowship Church in Spring Lake, Michigan. She holds a bachelor's degree in theology from Aquinas College, Grand Rapids, Michigan. Lembke lives with her husband, Charles, in Spring Lake, Michigan.

Other Titles Available
from FaithWalk Publishing

Into the Shadows: A Journey of Faith and Love into Alzheimer's
By Robert F. DeHaan ISBN: 0-9724196-3-2 $14.99

Homecoming: A Prophetic Study of Ruth
By Julie R. Wilson ISBN: 0-9724196-1-6 $16.00

Companions of Hope: A Study of Biblical Hope
By Julie R. Wilson ISBN: 0-9724196-5-9 $13.99

Daughter of Jerusalem: An American Woman's Journey of Faith
By Sharon Geyer ISBN: 0-9724196-2-4 $12.99

Vital Signs: The Promise of Mainstream Protestantism
By Milton J Coalter, John M. Mulder, Louis B. Weeks ISBN: 0-9724196-0-8 $12.99

Got the Time? A Search for Hope amidst Hopelessness
By Lori Gonzalez ISBN: 0-9724196-4-0 $11.99

The GodSense Devotional: 52 Weeks to a Transformed Life
By Beverly Van Kampen ISBN: 0-9724196-6-7 $13.99

The Disciple-Making Church: From Dry Bones to Spiritual Vitality
By Glenn McDonald ISBN: 0-9724196-8-3 $14.99

The Samson Option
by Sharon Geyer ISBN: 0-9724196-7-5 $12.99